Guests, Ho
the Holy Ghost

Who Tolkien's Tom Bombadil and
Goldberry are and why it really matters

Daniel Côté Davis and Michael Organ

The Spirit and the bride say, "Come!" And let the one who hears say, "Come!" Let the one who is thirsty come; and let the one who wishes take the free gift of the water of life.

- Revelations 22:17

Daniel Côté Davis - Daniel is a teacher, artist and poet. He has worked for the Canonisation of J.R.R. Tolkien in the Roman Catholic tradition through organising Conferences, Masses that have been held in Oxford (with Tolkien's granddaughter present), New York, Mexico and Canada, as well as spreading a prayer for private devotion to J.R.R. Tolkien in 7 languages. Daniel helped organise the More Than Memory Tolkien: Sacramental Imagination Conference at St Margaret's College, University of Oxford in 2019 and is helping to organise the Tolkien Conference: Heroic Virtue 2021 at Exeter College, University of Oxford. He is also co-founder of Silverion Camps Ltd., a Catholic medieval fantasy camp for youth in New Zealand, which takes as a source of inspiration Tolkien's sacramental vision and which he hopes will spread around the world through the Tyburn monasteries.

Michael Organ – Michael is a professional archivist and historian. He was the former University Archivist at the University of Wollongong, Australia, working there for thirty years and, as the Manager of Repository Services, promoting free online access to research publications and assisting in exposing the archival collections. His research interests include aspects of the work of J.R.R. Tolkien, pop culture and counterculture, art history and local history, having published in those areas within academic journals and books. He is also an inveterate blogger. During 2002-4 Michael served in the Australian federal parliament as a member of the Greens. He is a long-term advocate for Aboriginal heritage, culture, and self-determination. He also describes himself as something of a pacifist and is passionate about raising awareness of ecological concerns.

Abbreviations

HME   *The History of Middle-earth*, various volumes

Letter   Published letter in *The Letters of JRR Tolkien*

LOTR   *The Lord of the Rings*

Acknowledgements

Daniel: I would like to thank my family, Michael Caroll, Sr Therese, Mother Marilla, Adam and Samina Bukhari, Christopher Rogers and Pierre Ingram. You all helped me to understand the mysterious presence of the Holy Spirit. Thank you to David Sherwood for his support, Sophie Hobbs for giving me hope and Mark Holden for helping me follow my dreams. Many thanks to "E" who shuts out the night, and who made this book possible. I am eternally grateful to all of you and the thousands more who have helped me in the journey under myriad stars. *Michael*: I would like to thank my family for all their love and support. Also, the vast Tolkien fandom for their realisation of the enigmatic significance of Tom Bombadil and Goldberry. And finally, of course, to J.R.R. Tolkien and the Tolkien Estate for providing us with a world of wonder and meaning.

Cover image: Ironika (Photographer Videographer) / License: Shutterstock.

Cover design: vikncharlie, UK.

Contents

Foreword

By Joseph Pearce

Many of the most important things in life are mysteries, including the mystery of life itself. Is there a God? If so, who or what is God? Can he reveal himself? Does he reveal himself? How does he reveal himself? These mysteries are not merely an integral part of life on earth, they are also an integral part of life in Middle-earth.

According to its author, *The Lord of the Rings* is "a fundamentally religious and Catholic work". This is itself a mystery. How can *The Lord of the Rings* be fundamentally religious and Catholic when there is no mention of Christ or the Church anywhere in its pages? How can it be Catholic when the story takes place several millennia before the coming of Christ? Tolkien answers these questions but does so in such a paradoxically enigmatic and beguiling way that he merely adds to the mystery:

The Lord of the Rings is of course a fundamentally religious and Catholic work; unconsciously so at first, but consciously in the revision. That is why I have not put in, or have cut out, practically all references to anything like "religion", to cults or practices, in the imaginary world. For the religious element is absorbed into the story and the symbolism.

This subsumed religious element surfaces in the form of allegorical techniques that Tolkien learned from his medieval mentors. The authors of Beowulf and Sir Gawain and the Green Knight employ numerological or chronological signifiers to bring analogous religious applicability to the surface. In Beowulf, numerological signifiers are employed to connect Beowulf's fight with the dragon with the Passion of Christ. In Sir Gawain and the Green Knight, chronological signifiers are employed to connect key moments in the plot with key dates in the liturgical year. Tolkien knew both these works very well, of course, translating both into modern English. In *The Lord of the Rings*, he employs this technique by affixing the date of the Ring's destruction to the Feast of the Annunciation and to the traditional date ascribed to Christ's Crucifixion. The Ring is destroyed, therefore, on the date (March 25) on which God becomes man in the womb of the Virgin and the date on which he dies for our sins. These two events, taken together with the Resurrection, constitute Christ's triumph over sin in general and Original Sin in particular, the latter of which is the one sin to rule them all and in the darkness bind them. The one Sin and the one Ring are both destroyed on the same theologically charged date.

This is but one example, though perhaps the most potent and important. Tolkien employs many other adroit and subtle ways of subsuming the religious element into the story, far too many to enumerate here. One of the most enigmatic and often overlooked is the appearance of Tom Bombadil and Goldberry. Tom is a mystery. He is the eldest creature in Middle-earth, older than the Ents, much older than the elves. He is even older than the rivers and the trees, and the weather itself, remembering the first raindrop and the first acorn. He seems to be older than sin itself, being in Middle-earth "before the Dark Lord came from Outside".

He also appears to be immune to the seductive and destructive power of the Ring. When he puts it on, he doesn't disappear; when Frodo puts it on, Tom can still see him. Far from fearing it, he laughs at it. Far from being a character who can safely be ignored, he clearly possesses a power of his own, beyond that of the Ring itself, which commands not merely respect but reverence.

I endeavoured to get to grips with the elusive Tom and Goldberry in my book, *Frodo's Journey: Discovering the Hidden Meaning of The Lord of the Rings*, devoting a whole chapter to "the enigma of Tom Bombadil." I was aware when writing the chapter that I was only scratching the surface of the mystery. Someone needed to dive and delve deeper. Thankfully, Messrs. Davis and Organ, the authors of the present volume, have done just that. They have gone further up and further in, to employ the words of Aslan. They have gone much further up and further in than any previous scholars have ventured on the quest to discover the truths hidden in Tolkien's most elusive of mysteries.

Irrespective of whether Peter Jackson believed that Tom Bombadil and Goldberry could be safely left out of his film adaptation, no self-respecting admirer of Tolkien's work can afford to leave the present volume out of their reckoning and out of their reading. As Niggle proclaims in Tolkien's short story, Leaf by Niggle, "It's a gift!"

Read on and be dazzled by the brilliance of Tolkien and enlightened by the light that Tom and Goldberry shine forth. It's a gift!

Introduction

While walking across Spain to Santiago de Compostela I met, on my way, a Benedictine monk and he told me a story. He said there was once an abbot from his community who one day was so captivated by the sound of a bird in the forest on his daily walk, that he stood in awe and listened to its song. In all this he lost track of time and when he finally returned to his abbey, something strange had happened because the monks didn't know who he was. "I'm the abbot of this monastery" he said, and they shook their heads and said they did not know him. Getting frustrated the monk tried to convince everyone in the community but nobody believed him. Finally in exasperation he went to get the monastery's book of records, and to his shock and that of the other monks, his name was there, but they all said to him that it was several hundred years earlier! As I continued on my way towards my destination, I remained really curious about what I had learnt and still know today what that experience of curiosity feels like inside. Somehow, I knew this story was true, and I wanted to tell other people about this discovery. When I met Michael Organ, it was by recommendation from a guy who had made a documentary where he set out to find the J.R.R. Tolkien *The Lord of the Rings* character Tom Bombadil in the real world, travelling to many countries in search of his favourite person. I rang this guy on *WhatsApp* and tried to tell him that I knew where to find Tom. I was laughing with joy and felt what I had felt when that Benedictine monk told me his story, somewhere completely lost in the middle of Spain. This guy on W*hatsApp* said, "Go talk to Michael. He's researched everything about Tom." So, I did. Michael told me he was the kind of man who sometimes looked at clocks and thought, "Isn't it weird how sometimes, at specific times, I experience a coincidence and it's too startling to be random." I instantly liked him for the way he said that comment - it carried weight. I asked him if he thought that whatever Tolkien's Tom Bombadil was, his wife Goldberry was also. He said "yes," and, feeling like I had no choice, I said to him, "We must write this book." I also, as a result, committed to learn Morris dancing, and to pass it on to the next generation.

Daniel Côté Davis - August 2022

"Peace!" I said, holding up two fingers in support of this playground gesture. I was a twelve-year-old Catholic primary school kid at the time, back in 1968. Peace and love were the main messages I took from the nuns, the priests, the catechism lessons and the life of Jesus. All of that crystalised into those two words. At the time this refrain was all around me, in the music, the stories, the hippies and the hope of an end to conflict and a brave new world at one with the earth. I never understood the whole *spirit* thing that the nuns and priests talked about: The Holy Spirit / Holy Ghost, the Blessed Trinity, three persons in one God. That was 1968. Jump forward fifty years later to 2018. I am now a big fan of Peter Jackson's *The Lord of the Rings* movies. I vaguely remember reading *The Hobbit* back in 1969, and the trilogy the following year. But in 2018 the internet was here now, and I came across something strange – numerous J.R.R. Tolkien fans sites that talked about how good the Jackson trilogy was, but often with a caveat regarding a missing section at the beginning of *The Fellowship of the Ring*. Apparently, it added nothing to the narrative, so was left out. This intrigued me and set me on the path to understand: Why would Jackson and the other screenwriters omit three early chapters from the book? This brought me to the mysterious, mystical and enigmatic Tom Bombadil, and his partner Goldberry. I then began an intense period of research into Tom, and to a lesser extent Goldberry, looking for any and everything I could find – what Tolkien wrote or said about them, and what others had said since then. I discovered why the two characters did not fit the simple narrative thread loved by filmmakers. And I connected with that, for life is never a simple narrative. It is always full of complexity, diversity, and encounters with things that just don't fit, but nevertheless have meaning. And, somewhat surprisingly, I came to understand what that *spirit* thing from my youth was all about. Tolkien's publications, his letters and manuscripts, and the numerous discussions they engendered, brought me to an understanding of the Holy Spirit and the Catholic core of his vast legendarium. I also met, along the way, Danny, an English theologian then living in New Zealand – a modern day Middle-earth and home of Peter Jackson's production facilities. My somewhat simple, naïve understanding of Tom and Goldberry was on a level in many ways removed from Danny's intense and complex perspective. Yet, we could still communicate, if not in words, then in the mere knowledge that we appreciated the significance of what Tolkien had achieved. For though the filmmakers, general public and even die-hard fans often did not *get it*, Tolkien had laid out, in his distinctly convoluted manner, who and, more importantly, what these two characters were. This book unpacks the enigma and reveals why they, through acts of grace, played no small part in the ultimate defeat of Sauron and destruction of the Ring of Power.

Michael Organ – August, 2022

CHAPTER 1:

Who did we just meet?

W hy would one walk 800km across Spain? It is kind of random if it does not have any meaning. A lot of people have walked across Spain, but nowadays it is mostly walking enthusiasts who set out from the French Pyrenees for the cathedral of Santiago de Compostela and then beyond to the poetic Finisterre. That name literally means *the end of the earth*. It feels poetic to do so, as you know deep down that people have walked these roads all the way into the intangible past. Today you can walk the whole way without a map, as people have painted yellow arrows all across the country showing you where to go. Sometimes you're completely lost, and then your heart leaps as you spot the faint markings of the next arrow. You're really thirsty, but the arrow means you are more likely to refill your water bottle soon if you follow it. It is unknown for people to trick pilgrims by malicious false arrows, all of which is pretty amazing if you consider that this is the case for the whole length of a country.

What sort of spirit is behind all this? What spirit led the pagans who set out to see the setting sun over the horizons of the sea, and later Saint James who came over to Spain after the Resurrection of Jesus Christ to spread the Gospel? He was buried on the site of pilgrimage under the later cathedral of Santiago, built to honour him and of which pilgrims have set out from all corners of the world to reach for thousands of years. What is this all about?

If you walk 800km across Spain, it is definitely something you cannot really prepare for. Everybody says the same thing - the whole experience becomes so unexpected that it has a kind of magic to it. You can't put your finger on it, but you want to do it again and all you are really doing is walking. But the people you meet, and the gracious hospitality given to you by complete strangers, feels each time to be a sort of miracle. One is more open to miracles if all you are doing is just walking every day. It makes you more observant than usual, or observant in a different way to how you usually are, which might be the way you explain it.

At some point you sit down round a table with 20 other complete strangers who have made it to the albergue - intentional guest houses for pilgrims that are scattered all along the way and staffed by volunteers. One night the host washed my feet in a 12th century stone building, under the blanket of billions of stars. The table was candlelit and there was a lady walking round the table. She had come from Italy, in her own holiday, to pour, for any guest that came through the door, the "best wine she had produced" from her sun kissed vineyard, located somewhere "very beautiful," she said. I didn't know where it came from but it tasted sublime.

I never saw these two hosts again, but that night around the table we were all one, in a sort of communion together. It is like a big dance where everyone just knows that night only, and has never been taught. There is cheer, singing breaks out, and it feels like the strangest thing on earth. You look at these "strangers" around the table, but they don't look like strangers at all. In fact, they are almost more familiar than your own family. In the candlelight it feels like you are swimming inside a high-resolution image of a dream you might wake up from and be disappointed was not real - but it is real. You get back "home," but you are like, "that was more my home, more than here when I am back." You think about it in your memory and whilst you know it did happen, time is weird and you are like, "Did I just step into the future in that moment in the albergue? Is it possible to just wander into a plane of existence that was more real than anything on earth?" This all sounds unnecessarily esoteric, but if you do not believe it is possible, then walk 800km across Spain, and come back and try and explain what happened. Did not Jesus Christ say: *"The Kingdom of Heaven is now"*?

To encounter a French monk, like the one mentioned in the Introduction, reminds one of a very ancient story about Abraham, the founder of the Jewish religion. One day he hosted three guests. He fed them a proper meal and gave them drinks (Genesis 18). But he did something weird before this - he prostrated himself on the ground because he knew his guests were sacred and he was in awe of them. He felt there was no other response to seeing them that would have worked. Later interpretations of this story argue that his guests were angels, or they were even the God of Israel himself. You can check out the Rublev Icon which some consider the greatest piece of art of all time. It portrays three angels inviting you to share their table. Between their trifold gaze you are caught up in the dynamism of loving presence and it somehow takes all of you into the picture itself (Rublev 2017). It is like you are with them, in them.

People argue that the icon is a depiction of the Holy Trinity - three persons in one God. The whole point of the Trinity is that "God is Love" (John 1:8). Love is relational and so you need two persons - a Father and a Son. But their love is so personal, it is claimed it is a third person - the Holy Spirit, also known as the Holy Ghost. This love is timeless.

The whole cosmos did not have to happen. This is reflected when the question is asked: Why did God make the giraffes? And an answer is given, "Well, it was just for the hell of it." Look at a giraffe again and you might see what is meant by this claim. The point about the Blessed Trinity is that the love that chose to make everything, did so in complete freedom. Peace, it seems, is working out that this love is true. Listen to the majority of pop songs and it does seem to be the case that this is what it is all about - love. Snap back into history and by the time you get to the Christian letter to the Hebrews it gives the admonition which is worth considering:

Do not forget to show hospitality to strangers, for by so doing some people have shown hospitality to angels without knowing it. (Hebrews 13:2)

The title of this book is *Guests, Hosts and the Holy Ghost*. It is very curious to realise that the roots of the words "guest," "host" and "ghost" are arguably all related etymologically. A casual Google search will reveal this, although it is hotly debated. If you think of it, it is a crazy thing to try and explore. How could we definitely know what words existed, and meant, thousands of years ago, and especially before literature was a thing? It appears that it is worth trying, but still could we really know? We already know, for example, that in regards to the pronunciation of Anglo-Saxon, which is very easy to link to modern English, scholars simply have no idea what it was like during that period. This means that if we could meet an Anglo-Saxon, they probably would not be able to understand a word we were saying. In the Old Church Slavonic *gosti* means "guest, friend," and *gospodi* refers to "lord, master." Anybody who has stepped into a Divine Liturgy in full swing will hear again and again and again the refrain *Gospodi pomiluj*, which means *God have compassion on me*. The meanings of these three words are so intertwined that it seems the relationships of guests, hosts and Holy Ghost sink to the very core of what it means to exist in space and time. If one goes to a Divine Liturgy, you might even hear, or experience there in real-time, this incommunicable reality.

Human beings necessarily refer to their existence by narrative. All sentences that are composed tell a story, as self-consciousness is always a memory expressed. It gets crazy quickly when you think about talking about things in the future, as this is beyond the actual present. There is a Jesuit theologian called Karl Rahner who tries to get around this problem by saying that to be a human is to have a pre apprehensive grasp of the absolute (Coffey 2004). In other words, before we apprehend anything, we know infinity. In fact, the knowing of infinity is what makes apprehending and all its possibilities possible. Rahner thinks that built into human nature itself is this sphere of a supernatural infinite gift, known theologically as *grace*. Therefore, wandering through life as a human being is to exist within a framework of being within the Being of Grace. In metaphysical anthropology, which is the study of the structures of human existence, such an ontological understanding can be found; an understanding of what the true nature of being is. As life must be communicated through the expression of a journey, speech necessarily becomes narratival; stories must emerge about all this being in Being! What sort of stories would you think might emerge? That is a very important question that this book tries to address.

Dash forward into the eve of the second millennium and the French artist Marcel Duchamp decides to create a very rich pun as part of a live art installation within his new exhibition. He makes little tin foil sweet wrappers that have printed on them: "guest + host = ghost" (Duchamp 1953). This is only three words, but the statement works on so many levels. As Duchamp was raised a Catholic, this artwork opened up a bunch of other meanings beyond the guest-host relationship that is a social transaction as old as the first self-conscious humans. Hospitality is literally a lifeline. Think about it. Without hospitality agreed on socially, there is no society, no culture, no nation and no global community as is expressed in our modern technologically advanced world. Today's guest is tomorrow's host. But Duchamp cleverly brings in "ghost" as the mathematical conclusion of the "guest" and "host" and in doing so annihilates that relationship in the reality that every living thing dies. The Catholic Duchamp knows the word "host" carries both the meaning of the sacrificial victim on the altar of the Catholic Mass who is God, and also the Biblical meaning of "God Lord of Hosts" by which is meant the angel armies of Adonai the God of Israel. The annihilated "ghost" therefore in Duchamp's pun is also playfully intertwined with the Holy Ghost, who is the source of eternal life. All of this is found on a shiny tin foil sweet wrapper handed out to strangers walking into an exhibition. That is probably the best pun you could write. Who said that modern artists were 'degenerate'?

It is also possible to meet another monk, this time in France, in a community in the French countryside called Taizé. This is if he is still alive today. He had been met thousands of times, though his name is quite forgotten. This community was set up after World War II to inspire peace by inviting young people from around the whole world to stay as guests in basically what could be described as a hippie-commune-monastery located out amongst sunflower fields. The young people come in their thousands from every corner of the earth. They are known to sing *Gospodi Pomiluj* at three in the morning in the aeroplane hangar style chapel that is complete with Orthodox looking minarets. You can also find violins being played in the moonlight, as people who have never met, and will probably never meet again, dance and dance and dance. The young people take turns to serve each other their meals and drinks. This happens without any apparent intentional logistics, but it always works out. In reference to the old Taizé monk, he has been known by many to wander around the monastery looking out for tin foil sweet wrappers. He always found them and when people saw him, he would talk to them about what he was doing. Each time that encounter left a mark on him. He then made collage artwork out of the tin foil wrappers and they were surprisingly beautiful. Sometimes he showed them to people but he didn't make much of a fuss about doing so. What would that old monk have thought of Duchamp's pun?

Pope Francis, born Jorge Mario Bergoglio, believes that teachers should know all about the mystery of walking, as in a trek 800 km across Spain. It is something he wanted teachers to teach their young and impressionable pupils. This is how he put it in 2008, whilst still a Cardinal, linking the idea in with characters from Tolkien's *The Lord of the Rings*:

Tolkien portrays in Bilbo and Frodo the image of man who is called to walk. His heroes know and enact, precisely by walking, the drama ... between good and evil. The walking man has within him the dimension of hope: he enters into hope. Throughout mythology and history, there resounds the echo of the fact that man is not a still, tired being, but is called to the journey, and if he does not enter into this dimension, he destroys himself as a person and becomes corrupted. (Bergoglio 2008)

That is a big claim. If you do not set out on the journey into another dimension of hope, you are going to end up getting corrupted. This is curious when you find out that after the destruction of the Ring of Power, or the One ring, Gandalf gives two names to Frodo and Sam:

And when the burial was over and the last song was ended there was a great feast in the hall... And then Gandalf arose and bid all men rise, and they rose, and he said: 'Here is a last hail ere the

25

feast endeth. Last but not least. For I name now those who shall not be forgotten and without whose valour nought else that was done would have availed; and I name before you all Frodo of the Shire and Samwise his servant. And the bards and the minstrels should give them new names: Bronwe athan Harthad and Harthad Uluithiad, Endurance beyond Hope and Hope unquenchable. (HME Sauron Defeated 1992)

Jordan Peterson, the famous apologist for "maps of meaning" as he puts it, says an almost identical thing when he talks about Abraham as being an older guy still living with his parents when God says to him, basically, "Move out, get a life, there's stuff to do!" (Peterson 2017). This is similar to what Gandalf says to Frodo before sending him on a quest into the very dimension of an eternal hope. Pope Francis, in a 2022 essay on storytelling, states that the journey is the most crucial thing you can undertake, once again with reference to Tolkien:

As Frodo, the main character in Tolkien's 'The Lord of the Rings,' says: 'The tales never end.' (Bergoglio 2022)

According to Pope Francis, in stepping out on the journey you are going to encounter something infinite along the way; something eternal and timeless. This leads us to Tolkien's two most enigmatic characters. Who could they be?

What *The Lord of the Rings* character has the ability to manipulate and control the mind like Obi Wan Kenobi in *Star Wars*; meditate for hours on end like a Tibetan monk; is unaffected by Sauron's Ring of Power - the "One ring to rule them all" - and able to make it disappear; can walk out in the rain and not get wet; twice saves the party of hobbits led by Frodo Baggins at the beginning of their journey to Mordor; is the oldest living being in Middle-earth, yet not of Middle-earth; was present at the point of creation of Arda and all else in the universe; through song and speech has the power of creation; can provide the gift of life; can instil sleep, dreams and visions in others; is telepathic; is in love with a water spirit; appears to lead an idyllic life, though also exhibits a melancholy sadness from the weight of time and memory of things past; is fatherless; is nameless though has many names, including Master; can travel through space; can manipulate time; communicates with sentient beings including plants (trees) and animals; overflows with an innate goodness and joy; is grace personified; appears to be both spirit and corporeal; is immortal; and, at the end of *The Lord of the Rings*, following the defeat of Sauron and destruction of the Ring of Power, sees Gandalf the White seeking his counsel?

And furthermore, what *The Lord of the Rings* character has the ability to shut out demons by closing a door; host guests in a way that inspires rapture, dreams and longing; is unaffected by Sauron's Ring of Power and able to resist it inside her own home; has a name that implies she is younger than water but also the brightest and most precious fruit of sweetness; lives with, and marries, the oldest living being in Middle-earth; knows he who was

27

present at the point of creation of Arda and all else in the universe; through song and speech has the power of exorcism, holding a candle to banish demons; can provide the gift of rest and rejuvenation; can instil sleep, dreams and visions in others; is so mystical that she is arguably unknown to the Council of Elrond; is in love with a timeless being; appears to lead a paradisiacal life; receives constant gifts from her husband of beautiful water lilies, always with a renewed enthusiasm of wonder; is of unknown origin; is known only by one simple name; gets married mantled by the beauty of creation, with forget-me-nots and flag-lilies for garland and robed all in silver-green; embodies eternal youth; communicates with sentient beings including plants (trees) and animals; overflows with an innate goodness and joy; is grace personified; appears to be both spirit and corporeal; is immortal; and, when Gandalf goes to visit her husband at his home at the end of *The Lord of the Rings*, it is also her home, and one that is graced by an unaffected, timeless and peaceful spirit?

The answer is Tom Bombadil and his beloved wife Goldberry. Together they abide peacefully on the Barrow-Downs adjacent to the Old Forest, the latter of which abuts upon the Shire. In marriage they have become One; they are as the Catholic Mass states in the Eucharistic Prayer IV, echoing the Last Prayer before Christ's crucifixion - "gathered into one body by the Holy Spirit" (Roman Missal 2010). The mystery of the union of Tom Bombadil and Goldberry is so evident. Indeed, because of their oddness, they could easily be labelled divine beings in Arda (Earth), and the evocation of the Catholic Blessed Trinity. But most specifically of the three persons, they can be associated with the Holy Ghost or Holy Spirit, that which is by its very nature both peace and love, and through which the exorcistic function of destroying the dominion of the Devil is made possible.

Guests, Hosts and the Holy Ghost elucidates the argument that individually, and in union, Tom Bombadil and Goldberry is/are the personification of the Holy Ghost / Holy Spirit in Middle-earth. They are, as a consequence, enigmatic, mysterious, odd and unique characters within J.R.R. Tolkien's published works and wider legendarium. We also find mention of Tom and Goldberry in correspondence and manuscripts which remained unpublished during the author's lifetime.

In seeking to answer seemingly unanswerable questions as to who and what Tom Bombadil is, and in turn Goldberry, the task has been made almost impossible - and meaningfully so - by Tolkien himself, for not only did he alter the characters during his lifetime, both consciously and unconsciously, but he was especially reticent in elucidating Tom Bombadil's essence, preferring, instead, that he remain enigmatic. This may, in part, reflect the fact that Bombadil was also that to the author.

Herein we present, in some detail, aspects of Tom Bombadil's evolution from a 1934 children's verse character to the discordant, yet powerful Middle-earth figure seen within *The Lord of the Rings* and beyond. A complex nature is revealed, alongside the important role played by Tom and, to a lesser extent Goldberry, in the quest to destroy Sauron's Ring of Power. The specific in-depth analysis of Tom Bombadil is subsequently followed by a deeper, theological reflection on Goldberry, reflecting Tolkien's Catholic core and intimate attachment to his wife Edith (1916-71).

John Ronald Reuel Tolkien, born on 3 January 1892, was baptised according to the Tridentine Rite, with water poured over his head three times, his baby face lit by a gleaming light of a candle held by his mother Mabel. He would have heard, but never fully remembered, coming from the priest's mouth the following words:

In virtute Spiritus sancti. Exorcizo te per Deum vivum, per Deum verum, per Deum sanctum...ut in nomine sanctae Trinitatis efficiaris salutare sacramentum ad effugandum inimicum. [In the power of the Holy Spirit, I exorcise you by the living God, by the true God, by the holy God... that in the name of the Holy Trinity you may become a salutary sacrament to flee the enemy.] (Ordo Baptismi Parvulorum 1962)

This is where our story begins....

CHAPTER 2:

Where did you get your energy from?

E verything in being has energy. That is what scientists are observing on the nano level. But where did that energy come from? How did energy come to exist? Can that question even be answered? When J.R.R. Tolkien was baptised, according to Catholic theology the very energy that created him - known as the Holy Spirit or Holy Ghost - invited him into being the guest *of a new dimension of hope*. According to that theology, the host of the baptism - the Catholic Priest - stands through the Holy Ghost in the Person of Jesus Christ himself. Wherever one person of the Blessed Trinity is, the two others are also, as they are so inseparable as to be always present as One, in the form of God the Father, God the Son, or the Word of God (Logos), and God the Holy Spirit, or Holy Ghost.

This priest conferred actual grace to the baby Ronald he baptised, opening up the doors of Heaven as the destination for this little earthly creature wriggling in Mabel's arms. Having been marked by this baptism, which leaves an unshakeable spiritual mark akin to Jewish circumcision in its significance, Tolkien was a changed creature. It seems quite likely that the Person of the Holy Spirit would arrive somewhere in his writings to offer an invitation into the *new dimension of Hope* that the child had received. In a letter written in 1956, Tolkien described this process in his own words, taking the idea right to its end in an incredible conclusion often entirely overlooked:

The Other Power then took over: the Writer of the Story (by which I do not mean myself), 'that one ever-present Person who is never absent and never named'. (Letter 192)

This can be compared to his 1955 letter to English author and poet W.H. Auden, once again referring to himself in the role of writer:

I met a lot of things on the way that astonished me. Tom Bombadil I knew already; but I had never been to Bree. Strider sitting in the corner at the inn was a shock, and I had no more idea who he was than had Frodo. The Mines of Moria had been a mere name; and of Lothlorien no word had reached my mortal ears till I came there. Far away I knew there were the Horselords on the confines of an ancient Kingdom of Men, but Fangorn Forest was an unforeseen adventure. I had never heard of the House of Eorl nor of the Stewards of Gondor. Most disquieting of all, Saruman had never been revealed to me, and I was as mystified as Frodo at Gandalf's failure to appear on September 22. (Letter 163)

In writing the current book, the authors came to believe that in *The Lord of the Rings,* through the characterisation of Tom Bombadil and his 'River-daughter' wife Goldberry, one can find an apotheosis of the Divine Energy as a Person that inspired Tolkien's creative vision. This Person is the Holy Ghost, who "took over" and helped Tolkien write his story, as his letter attests, and also came to dwell within the narrative as the hidden key to unlocking the defeat of evil within that story. It would make sense that the Holy Ghost within Middle-earth would be known before any of Middle-earth was even invented in the professor's mind, as the Holy Spirit is the Being that brought all beings into existence. Tolkien didn't even use the word 'invent' for his Middle-earth, but rather that he "discovered" it. Even as he talks about the germs of the characters he came to meet as he wrote, Tom Bombadil he said *he already knew.* In fact, we think you can meet and encounter the Holy Ghost therein and find an invitation into receiving the gifts offered by this Person. That is what we want to try and inspire readers to receive through this book. We have no idea how we could inspire such a thing to happen, but felt compelled to. That such an opportunity would be possible, would be due to the grace received by virtue of that Tridentine baptism as occurred when the professor himself was just a little baby. That grace was a seed which has now germinated into a great tree of Middle-earth itself. As the parable Jesus told goes, and which Tolkien called *The Haeland* (Saviour in Old English):

The kingdom of Heaven is like a mustard seed that a man planted in his field. Although it is the smallest of all seeds, yet it grows into the largest of garden plants and becomes a tree, so that the birds of the air come and nest in its branches. (Matthew 13:31-32)

Tolkien received and shared this tree, and Tom Bombadil was there from the beginning of it all. As also was Goldberry, by means of the union of their marriage which, according to Catholic theology, is a sacrament making a new creation and a Divine and inseparable bond. Both in Tolkien's mind and also in reality itself, the Holy Ghost is the beginning and the end, the "Alpha and the Omega", as the Easter prayer says (Roman Missal, 2010). Tolkien is also clear in this regard:

Tom was here before the river and the trees; Tom remembers the first raindrop and the first acorn. He made paths before the Big People, and saw the little People arriving. He was here before the Kings and the graves and the Barrow-wights. When the Elves passed westward, Tom was here already, before the seas were bent. He knew the dark under the stars when it was fearless before the Dark Lord came from Outside. (LOTR)

Questions arise from this reflection of the Person of the Holy Spirit as being personified by Tom Bombadil and his wife, which to our mind are meaningfully apparent. Such questions are:

Q1: Imagine you could be given happiness, peace and joy forever. If you knew it was possible, would not you give up everything you had just to receive this wonderful gift?

Q2: Imagine, if it was completely free and the only thing you would have to do is ask for it, would not you jump at the chance immediately?

Tolkien from a young age became aware of this sort of possibility in life, where such an unbelievable gift was being offered to him personally. As a lover of words, he mined their hidden meaning to share as treasure in his stories, and within them the secrets of the wondrous gift he received are shared with those who have the eyes to see. Raised in the Catholic Faith by his mother and later when adopted by Oratorian priests, Tolkien from a young age learnt by heart the key beliefs of the *Penny Catechism*. That whole little book could be summed up in these simple words about the meaning of life:

To know, love, and serve God, and to be happy with Him forever in Heaven. (Penny Catechism 2009)

It is impossible to understand Tolkien's art without realising that this Catholic Faith was so natural to him. In fact, when Catholics say that something is supernatural what they mean is that something is so natural that you might say it was infinitely natural and without limit. In this way, you could think of Tolkien's faith as being like a hobbit hole - the place where he was most naturally

35

at home in the world, but also as something supernatural because he knew this little home on earth was only the beginning of an adventure whose final destination was Heaven, an eternal home. Restless like Bilbo, he thought we could hear the call that, as our hobbit holes are not completely satisfactory, there is still something greater out there to be sought after and not a moment to lose. This is why Tolkien in his life journey received all the sacraments of the Catholic Church. According to his faith, these seven gifts of God are given freely, to help all human beings who want to reach happiness, peace and joy forever and to reach Heaven.

To achieve the goal of this journey of hope, Tolkien was baptised as a baby, meaning he was freed from the curse of the Devil and made a child of God. Later, he was confirmed by a bishop as a teenager, to assure him of his faith. He married in the Catholic Church and made a sacred vow to his wife Edith for life. He regularly experienced mercy when confessing his sins and receiving absolution from a priest washing the presence of evil from his heart. One of his sons received Holy Orders and became a Catholic priest who was able to bring God down from Heaven and onto a human-built altar. When he was sick, Tolkien received Last Rites to prepare him for the final journey to Heaven and, most importantly to him, from a young age he came to know Jesus literally present, according to his faith, in the Blessed Sacrament. This Bread from Heaven was for him, by virtue of his faith, the literal presence of God on earth, and was both his hobbit hole but also his true home in the Undying Lands. It was the beginning and the end of the journey at the same time. Tolkien was an altar server and later experienced a vision of his guardian angel in front of the Blessed Sacrament, pointing out to him the infinite presence of God. He encouraged people to go to Mass daily and he loved the Virgin Mary deeply and described her as the inspiration of any beauty he created. All these things made Tolkien who he was, and it would be impossible to understand anything that he created without knowing his hidden identity as a man who lived his Catholic faith fully.

The paradox at the heart of this book is that in welcoming the Holy Ghost / Holy Spirit an individual is actually being welcomed and hosted as a special guest *by* the Person of the Holy Ghost / Holy Spirit. In fact, what could be better than shutting out the night, a good bath, the promise of a hearty meal filled with mystery and wonder, and the assurance that everything will be alright as long as you always call for help that will come? We do not honestly think anything is better, and that is why we want to invite you to come along with us for the quest where we will encounter, and be hosted by, the most beautiful and simple Person.

CHAPTER 3:

An Enigmatic Oddity

enigma (noun) a person or thing that is mysterious or difficult to understand.

odd (adjective) a person or thing differing from all others, strange.

He's a mystery character. He's a magical character. He has no background. He comes and goes. He's the subversive secret mysterious stranger that enters the film and then exits at the end.
(George Lucas on Yoda)

We know who Tom Bombadill is – he is a character created by J.R.R. Tolkien, and he plays an important role in the early chapters of *The Lord of the Rings*. However, when we ask the question: *What is Tom Bombadil?* we find that the author provides us with no simple answer. He just does not seem to fit. Relating him to the Christian God has occurred within fandom. However, therein it is generally believed, due to equivocating statements from Tolkien himself, that "God", and indeed the lesser "gods", are absent from *The Lord of the Rings,* though dealt with elsewhere in some detail within Tolkien's copious writings. As such, many commentators briefly discuss this possibility, then dismiss it. There appears only one example where it is supported, or rather, strongly suggested, and that is in an anonymous Mormon blog (RJH 2013).

Tolkien, when queried about this superficial omission of God and gods from *The Lord of the Rings* by the BBC interviewer Denys Gueroult in 1964, pointed to his meaningful rejection of the idea of utilising traditional Greco-Roman gods, or the like, within his mythology-based legendarium:

Gueroult: *Where is God in The Lord of the Rings?*

Tolkien: *Mentioned once or twice....*

Gueroult: *Is he the One, mentioned above all others?*

Tolkien: *The One .... Yes.... God is supreme, the creator, outside, transcendent.... But the place of the "gods" is taken by the angelic spirits created by God, created before the particular time sequence which we call the World, which is called in their language "Eä" i.e., that which is, that which now exists. Those are the Valar – the power. It is a construction of geo-mythology in which a large part of the demiurgic [creation] of things has been handed over to powers that are created therein under the One.*

Gueroult: *Therefore, you have in your theocracy an ultimate One whom you call...*

Tolkien: *The One only.*

Gueroult: *The One only, and then the Valar who are considered as living in Valinor...* (Gueroult and Tolkien 1964)

The legendarium was Tolkien's equivalent to the modern-day Marvel Cinematic Universe (MCU), and an example of world-building. He replaced Zeus and what we at present refer to as superheroes with unique, and original, god-like beings in the form of Ainur, Valar and Maiar.

Tom Bombadil's status as either *the* Christian God, a pagan god, a lesser divine being within the legendarium, or the extraordinary creation deemed by Tolkien important, necessary and even somewhat "odd" within *The Lord of the Rings*, does not explain or justify the fact that he is more often than not omitted from adaptations of the novel and associated commentaries, on the misplaced pretext that his role therein is irrelevant to the narrative. This was recognised by Tolkien himself, and perhaps meaningfully made to appear so. Bombadil's exclusion from the Peter Jackson films, for example, generated much criticism at the time of their initial release commencing in 2001. Unfortunately, film is very much driven by the need for a concise narrative. Stripping away elements which do not drive that narrative forward is a common part of the modern-day editorial process, even if it detracts from character development and world-building. The exclusion of Tom Bombadil and Goldberry has subsequently been rationalised in many forms by Jackson and others, though the omission remains a sore point with some fans and, in the view of the current authors, rightfully so (Bogstad & Kaveny 2012, Middle-earth Lore 2019, Nathan 2015). Jackson was not alone in this process of exclusion. Bombadil had been left out of the 1978 Ralph Bakshi animated adaptation of the first half of *The Lord of the Rings*, along with various radio plays produced even earlier (Korkis 2003). The excision continues and has almost become embedded in Tolkien lore, due to the ongoing influence of the Jackson films. As recently as October 2020, an online account of the travels of Gandalf mentioned Tom Bombadil at the very end, and then only briefly (Nerd of the Rings 2020).

There has literally been one significant exception to the regrettable omission, and that only came to light in April 2021 when the 115 minute long, 1991 Russian television adaptation of Book 1 of *The Lord of the Rings,* entitled *Krhaniteli* [*Keepers of the Ring*], appeared on YouTube (Serebryakova 1991). Therein some 22 minutes featured Tom Bombadil, Goldberry, Old Man Willow and the Barrow-wights in scenes adapted from the original text. Needless to say, despite the quirkiness of the presentation and its low budget nature, their inclusion at the beginning of the film revealed, as Tolkien would have wished, the importance of the role played by Tom Bombadil and Goldberry in empowering and emboldening the hobbit party, and also in saving them from fates not only worse than death, but actual death in some cases.

One reason for Bombadil's omission elsewhere from the public audio-visual presentations is that Tolkien presented him as a superficially jolly character who, at least upon first reading, seemed not to be significant in the quest to destroy the Ring of Power. A deeper reading of the published text, plus Tolkien's draft notes and subsequent correspondence, reveals the case to be otherwise, as Bombadil's aforementioned abilities and actions affected change to the innocent and ignorant party of hobbits as they set out upon their quest. One commentator has referred to Tom as a *deus ex machina* (God in the Machine) i.e., a plot device whereby the seemingly unsolvable problem of enabling the hobbit party led by Frodo Baggins to destroy the Ring of Power is suddenly and abruptly resolved by an unexpected and unlikely occurrence, in the form of their encounter with Tom Bombadil and Goldberry (Lockett 2014, Wikipedia 2021). Gollum could also be said to serve as a similar device. By ignoring this section of the story, and with only a superficial understanding of the text prevailing, Bombadil could therefore easily be omitted from any truncated presentation of the book without impacting upon the flow of the narrative in regard to the quest to destroy the Ring of Power. Any such edited version would not address the issue of the transformation of a group of timid hobbits into beings who played a large part in the defeat of Sauron. Such editorial omissions nevertheless evidence a failure on the part of those responsible to understand, or investigate, the true nature of Bombadil and Goldberry, and Tolkien's intent in creating a complex cosmology within his work, wherein underlying Christian values and themes dominate.

Tom Bombadil is a distinctly solitary figure within *The Lord of the Rings*, apart from attachment to his wife – the likewise enigmatic Goldberry, who in many ways mirrors the presence and power of her husband. Superficially, Bombadil merely appears to offer adventure on the way for the party of hobbits led by Frodo Baggins, much as Beorn did to Bilbo Baggins and the party of dwarves within *The Hobbit*. But, as with Beorn, there is much within the mystery surrounding the two characters. Bombadil can be read and understood on a variety of levels, from redundant buffoon to be ignored, to God-like manifestation of Tolkien's 'the One', and everything in between. At the core of the narrative abandonment of Bombadil by readers, commentators and filmmakers, is his dismissive attitude towards Sauron's Ring of Power. Bombadil's nonchalant attitude threatens to derail the noble quest at the very outset. For this reason alone, it is no wonder that the encounter is thought by many to be best forgotten. The question must therefore be asked: Why did Tolkien include Bombadil's offhand rejection of, and flippancy towards, the Ring of Power? Including it, immediately puts Bombadil at odds with Gandalf, the hobbit party led by Frodo Baggins, and the wider

Fellowship of the Ring. This episode also negates the main element driving the narrative forward and is therefore more easily ignored in the filmic environment rather than rationalised and included. Yet Tom Bombadil and Goldberry are powerful figures who provide essential protection, guidance and gifts to assist the hobbits at the outset of their quest. They are therefore characters of deep significance to *The Lord of the Rings* narrative, and within the mythological world created by Tolkien. This is not always, or easily, recognised, but it is there. Tolkien told us it is there.

According to one fan website, Tom Bombadil is '*the prevailing mystery in Tolkien's work*' (Encyclopaedia of Arda 2003); whilst to another he is '*the key to understanding Tolkien's worldview ... a character of great symbolic and spiritual depth*' (Denney 2012). If this is so, why is he ignored by many, treated as merely a comic interlude, or meaningfully excluded from retellings? Throughout the original published texts, the unpublished manuscripts, the later personal correspondences, the retellings, and the commentaries, Bombadil remains an enigma, having, unfortunately, meaningfully been made so by Tolkien. A possible reason for that is suggested within the context of this current discussion. However, in order to understand it, the reader must first be made aware of the more fulsome nature of Bombadil as revealed first hand by Tolkien. For we must ultimately base any view of Tom Bombadil upon what Tolkien wrote or said about him, and not on second-hand interpretations or suppositions.

Within *The Lord of the Rings* Tolkien focussed on the story of the destruction of the Ring of Power, not on the world of Tom Bombadil and his role in the greater legendarium, which indirectly extended beyond that book into the world of *The Hobbit* and *The Silmarillion*. Tom was there in substantial physical presence at the beginning of *The Lord of the Rings*, but not at the end, apart from a slight, though nevertheless significant footnote. Bombadil's interactions with the party of hobbits at the beginning of their quest reveal much about his character, as do later comments made at the secret Council of Elrond by Gandalf, Galdor and others who previously knew of, or about, him. However, the information provided therein is sketchy, if not intriguing, leaving the reader with numerous unanswered questions and a non-holistic portrait of the character.

Since Bombadil first appeared in *The Lord of the Rings* upon publication of *The Fellowship of the Ring* in July 1954 a variety of articles, blogs, audio-visual items and internet postings have attempted to deal with the mystery surrounding his true nature. Unfortunately, each of those usually provides a different interpretation of Tolkien's raw material, and there is no general consensus as to who or what he is. The list of commentaries is extensive (O'Neil 1979, Herbert 1985, Hargrove 1986, Jeffs 1987, Scull 1991, Shippey 2000, Jensen 2001, Stanton 2001, Loos 2002, Shippey 2003, Gay 2004, Noad 2004, Not all those who wander art lost 2004, Treschow & Duckworth 2006, Lewis 2007, Martin

2011, Martinez 2011, Panek 2011, SciFi & Fantasy 2011, Tolkien Gateway 2012, Quora 2015, In Deep Geek 2020, Nerd of the Rings 2021). Tom Bombadil would appear to be a timelessly intriguing character. One recent manifestation of this is the 2019 film *Finding Tom Bombadil* in which 'holistic detective' and film director Joost van de Loo goes looking for Tom Bombadil in the real world (van de Loo 2019a). In a 2021 posting to an online discussion forum which posed the question *Who is Tom Bombadil?*, one correspondent even likened him to Buddha (Nerd of the Ring 2021). This current study is another in the long line of quests to understand and unravel Tolkien's greatest enigma.

Why undertake such a quest? The answer is simple: because it may provide a key to a better understanding of Tolkien's larger legendarium – an alternate, idealised mythological world reflecting, and commenting upon, our own reality. In light of this, what is perhaps more achievable at the outset of this study, rather than attempting the seemingly impossible and ongoing quest by fans of *The Lord of the Rings* to grapple with the enigma that is Tom Bombadil, is the process of identifying what Tolkien actually wrote and said about him. In going down this path of discovery we can initially take the character for who he is, as described by the author, or who he became, rather than philosophising on what he could be, beyond what Tolkien cared to reveal. The first task is relatively straightforward, merely requiring research and compilation, though not everything that Tolkien wrote about

Bombadil is accessible, with some manuscripts in private hands and no published transcriptions available. This 'What is he?' effort, however, is fraught with difficulty and leads to confusion and variant opinion, for Tom Bombadil is a riddle in much the same manner as Lewis Carrol's unanswerable question from *Alice in Wonderland:* 'Why is a raven like a writing desk?' (Carroll 1865). Of course, there is no answer therein, and none provided by the deceptive Dodgson. Having said that, the writers of this study inevitably went down that latter, tortuous path, presenting herein conclusions as to what, rather than who, Tom Bombadil is. But first things first. What did Tolkien write, and say?

The character of Tom Bombadil, as presented within *The Lord of the Rings*, evolved over time, both within and beyond the realm of Middle-earth, as Tolkien refined his greater mythology during an extended period from 1913 through to his death in 1973 (Carpenter 1977). During that period Tolkien the writer did three things: (1) he constructed an incredibly complex legendarium, of which works such as *The Hobbit, The Lord of the Rings, The Book of Lost Tales* and *The Silmarillion* are part; (2) he wrote stories – for his children, and for a wider audience – which had nothing to do with the legendarium; and (3) he produced academic publications, including translations of classic texts such as *Beowulf.*

The character of Tom Bombadil initially appeared outside of the legendarium, and was ultimately inserted within. This is amply revealed in the analysis of the drafting of *The Lord of the Rings*

48

carried out by his son Christopher Tolkien (1924-2020) and substantially published as *The Return of the Shadow*, *The Treason of Isengard*, *The War of the Ring* and *Sauron Defeated*, all within the multi-volume *The History of Middle-earth* series (Tolkien 1983-96). The *Reader's Companion to The Lord of the Rings* and *The Reader's Guide* by Christina Scull and Wayne G. Hammond also provide useful references and analyses, being the best of a number of related analytical works which aid in unravelling the complex world of Tolkien's legendarium and the place of *The Lord of the Rings* within it (Foster 1978, Duriez 1992, Hammond and Scull 2002, Scull and Hammond 2006). Whilst a study of this evolutionary process as applied to Tom Bombadil can lead to confusion, there is also revelation, for it provides a rich tapestry which aids in better understanding the character's development over time. Much change did occur, though Tolkien was ultimately loath to reveal the rhyme or reason for that, and expand upon the presentation of the character at its most complex within *The Lord of the Rings*.

The story of Tom Bombadil begins, in part, during the late 1920s with the acquisition of a toy for the Tolkien children – John (b.1917), Michael (b.1920), Christopher (b.1924) and Priscilla (b.1929). This was in the form of a peg-wood Dutch doll which was then given the onomatopoeic name Tombombadil, or Tom Bombadil, a possible childish distortion of the word bombardier (Reynolds 1991). Originally owned by Michael, his older brother

John took a dislike to the toy and put it down the toilet, from whence their father retrieved it (Carpenter 1977, Beal 2018). The distinctive clothing of the subsequent literary creation - blue coat, yellow boots and blue cap with a feather - initially came from the doll. The origin of personal traits such as a long beard, bright blue eyes and a wrinkled, red face is not known, though they likely derive from the author's imagination and readings. The doll was obviously played with, and perhaps the focus of stories developed by Tolkien for his children. For example, at some point during the late 1920s the author was moved to write a brief piece of historical fantasy that contained the first mention of the character (Tolkien 2014). Therein references to being old, hale and hearty, and possessing a melodious voice, very much summed up Bombadil as the character evolved through to the 1960s. The prose also had aspects of rhythmic verse within it, especially evident in the final sentence. This was something the author would develop, most obviously in Bombadil's use of song. Additional to the brief text is an undated 23-line long verse that develops this musical aspect of the character, whilst placing him within a physical environment of an unspecific river. Building upon this, around 1931 Tolkien prepared some ornate Elvish (Tengwar) texts which included elements of what would become the more substantial verse *The Adventures of Tom Bombadil,* and which itself was earlier known as *The History of Tom Bombadil.* This work would form the foundation of the character as he eventually appeared in *The Lord of the Rings.* All of this points to the fact that Tom Bombadil was very much in the mind of Tolkien prior to his writing of his most famous work. As a result, he could, and would, look to make use of him if the opportunity arose.

In 1934, the first published and expanded version of the 1931 Tengwar narrative verse appeared in the *Oxford Magazine* as the approximately 120-line long verse *The Adventures of Tom Bombadil* (Tolkien 1934). It was later reissued during 1962 with minor amendments to bring it into line with *The Lord of the Rings*. The manuscript of that latter famous work had been started late in 1937 and completed in 1948, though it was not published until 1954-5. Tolkien also recorded the Bombadil verse on tape in 1967 (Popova 2016).

The 1934 version of *The Adventures of Tom Bombadil* reflected its origin as entertainment for children, with a rhyming structure and simple adventurous narrative based around the figure of Tom Bombadil, but also including Goldberry, Old Man Willow and a Barrow-wight. A possible literary precursor was the work of 12th century Scottish poet Thomas the Rhymer (Murray 1987). In that author's most famous tale a similarly named young man is kidnapped by an Elf queen, forced to produce rhyming verse, placed under a spell in which he cannot lie, and subject to the development of the gift of prophecy. Tolkien makes specific reference to Thomas the Rhymer in his 1939 lecture on fairy stories, presented around the time that the first chapters of *The Lord of the Rings* were being written (Tolkien 2008). Elements of this tale are therefore clearly reflected in the person of Tom Bombadil. Another possible inspiration is Poor Tom, a character in the William Shakespeare play *King Lear* (Shakespeare 1605). Poor Tom was a court jester and a fool who existed outside the normal social order. He is described as a figure of 'madness, poverty and linguistic play', characteristics which can be applied, in part, to Tom Bombadil and which are directly referenced in Tolkien's writings (Lee 2009). Another commentator equates him with G.K. Chesterton's Innocent Smith, the absurd sage and holy fool from the novel *Manalive* who cavorts through life awakening people to the beauty of the world and existence (Chesterton 1912, Long 2012).

The 1934 verse *The Adventures of Tom Bombadil* contained much that would define the character of Tom Bombadil and also appear later in *The Lord of the Rings*. This included the power to induce sleep, ward off evil, and influence the actions of others through speech and song (Bebb 2008). It also introduces Goldberry the river spirit as Tom's wife, forcibly taken in what appears to be playful revenge for her own previous capture of him; Old Willow Man, who visits the couple on their wedding night; and the wraith-like, spectral Barrow-wights. At no point did it describe what type of being Bombadil was. Likewise, Goldberry was only given as a River-woman's daughter. Both were figures of fantasy and not, at that stage, specifically part of Tolkien's developing Middle-earth legendarium. Neither were they precisely defined in time or space.

The character of Tom Bombadil remained in this form for a number of years whilst Tolkien was occupied with the publication of *The Hobbit* (Tolkien 1937). That text had been substantially completed by late 1932, less than two years prior to the appearance of *The Adventures of Tom Bombadil*. In turn, *The Hobbit* was subsequently published on 23 September 1937. It was an immediate success, bringing with it pressure for a sequel. On 16 December 1937, in a letter to his publisher Stanley Unwin which included an attached copy of the 1934 Tom Bombadil verse, Tolkien was fishing around for ideas and therein identified the character as a possible sequel subject, describing him as a type of contemporary earth spirit (Letter 19).

Bombadil was, at the time, an interesting character already developed to a degree, both in print and within Tolkien's imagination, with the potential for enlargement. He was therefore able to be used to fill up the blank pages that lay before him as he set out on 16 December 1937 to begin work on *The Hobbit* sequel. Tolkien would go on to use the Bombadil verse of 1934 as the basis for elements of this new work. During the last weeks of 1937 and through into the first half of 1938, he incorporated Bombadil within an evolving Middle-earth narrative. But things were also to change. In a letter written on 19 December 1937, and addressed to C.A. Furth of the firm of Allen & Unwin, Tolkien noted that he had begun writing the first chapter of what was to become *The Lord of the Rings* (Letter 19). However, the idea of making Tom

Bombadil the central hero of the story was now abandoned and replaced by a hobbit. Over the following six weeks to the end of January 1938, the first chapter quickly evolved through four different drafts. During this period Tolkien also developed a further two chapters and compiled additional notes referring to the inclusion of Tom Bombadil within the story.

The first brief notice of Bombadil, reproduced in Christopher Tolkien's *The History of Middle-earth: Return of the Shadow*, indicates that Tolkien made the decision very early on to include characters from the 1934 verse in *The Lord of the Rings* and enlarge the portrait of him therein. This would now include associated events in and around the Old Forest and Withywindle River, which was mapped out in detail and located adjacent to the Shire, home of hobbits. Tolkien, in his notes, also laid out what that inclusion would entail. More importantly, he knew that Tom could easily provide the hobbits with an adventure during the early stages of the book, at a point where its precise direction had not been determined. Tolkien had obviously given some thought to expansion of the role of Bombadil's character between publication of *The Hobbit* and commencing the first chapter of *The Lord of the Rings*. Despite the character ultimately being rejected as the book's focus, Bombadil was not abandoned altogether and would feature in these early chapters.

Tolkien later wrote that he felt the need to include Bombadil and leave him in as representative of *"certain things otherwise left out"*

(Letter 153). Precisely what this meant was not made clear through a straightforward reading of the book, though it was obviously clear to Tolkien in the writing, and remained so through to the book's eventual publication some sixteen years later. It also suggested that the character served as a repository for, and reflection of, ideas that arose during the course of compiling and editing the text. These were ideas and elements that Tolkien wanted included, but would not appear on the surface to be integral to the overriding narrative. So it was that the enigmatic nature of the character developed.

By the end of January 1938, the first three chapters of *The Lord of the Rings* had been written in draft form, along with an outline of incidents involving Tom Bombadil, the Old Forest and the mysterious Barrow-wights (Callahan 1972). After this initial flourish of writing, and as university work and family commitments took over, Tolkien put it all aside from February through to the middle of 1938. However, between 29 - 31 August he completed the work up to the beginning of what would ultimately become chapter VII, *In the House of Tom Bombadil*, with the account of Tom and his wife Goldberry expanded upon and now featured. As war with Germany came ever closer to Tolkien's homeland, and was ultimately declared on 3 September 1939, the new narrative began to reflect 'the darkness of the present days' in comparison with the light-hearted tone and children's book origin of its prequel (Letter 34). For example, in their early encounters with Bombadil, the hobbit party experiences both the lightness of his presence and the darkness of the world around, reflecting Tolkien's own feelings and experiences during the latter part of the 1930s as war came ever closer to home.

In undertaking a detailed study of what Tolkien wrote about Tom Bombadil in both manuscript and published form, it is helpful to look to specific events contained within *The Lord of the Rings* pertaining to him, and which provide context to the development of his character. The events of both *The Hobbit* and *The Lord of the Rings* take place within Tolkien's so-called Third Age, though both those texts make references to early time periods in passing.

With Tom Bombadil largely excised from popular adaptations of *The Lord of the Rings*, it is difficult to obtain a mind's eye picture of the character beyond a reading of the book and related items of verse. However, Tolkien's large fan base has, over time, resurrected him from obscurity, such that he now exists in a number of adapted forms, including figurines, artworks, within computer games, card games, and as the star of amateur online videos, and of course in the 1991 Russian television adaptation. Apart from that latter, an additional aid in visualising the Bombadil character can be found in the collection of animations associated with the 2007 *The Lord of the Rings* computer game (Tolkien Enterprises 2007). Whilst there is a lot of game play interwoven therein, digital representations of Tom and Goldberry provide a useful reference in the absence of definitive cinematic versions. In addition, an amateur, fan-produced 12-minute video of the encounter between Tom and the hobbits can also be found on YouTube, alongside numerous face-to-camera and audio-only discussions of the character. The majority of these offer opinions as to who he is and, more importantly, what he is, based on a distinction that Tolkien himself made (Barlow 2016, Geekzone 2017, Men of the West 2017, The Exploring Series 2017).

Beyond these pop culture references to Tom Bombadil, the early chapters of *The Lord of the Rings* feature detailed accounts of Tom, Goldberry and the party of hobbits that would ultimately comprise Frodo Baggins, Samwise Gamgee, Meriadoc 'Merry' Brandybuck and Peregrin 'Pippin' Took. The chapters therein were entitled: 'The Old Forest', 'In the House of Tom Bombadil' and 'Fog on the Barrow-downs'.

During the lengthy drafting of *The Lord of the Rings* between 1937-48, Tolkien re-wrote the various chapters on numerous occasions and attempted to bring a level of internal consistency to the people, places and events portrayed therein. It was a mammoth task. All the while he was bearing in mind the story's context within his greater legendarium, as later revealed through *The Silmarillion* and related works published after his death. As a result, the activities and character of Tom Bombadil evolved, with the most comprehensive and complex account of his experiences to be found in the final, published version of *The Lord of the Rings*. That material is core to any analysis of the character. The numerous references to Bombadil contained within the 3-volume omnibus edition of *The History of Middle-earth* record many of the changes applied by Tolkien during the drafting process.

In these early stages of writing during the second half of 1938, Tolkien was formulating what he would and would not say in regards to numerous characters, including Tom Bombadil, the Black Riders, Barrow-wights and Goldberry. In these drafts we can see the first signs of significant character development beyond what existed in the 1934 verse. For example, the idea of Bombadil's immortality is raised when we are informed that he is (1) very old, and (2) a type of master of the world around him. Tolkien even uses the term 'Aborigine', which implies an attachment to the local place as an original inhabitant, prior to the coming of Middle-earth creatures such as men, elves, hobbits and dwarves. Tolkien at one point altered this to Ab-origine which, in Latin, means 'at the beginning' and suggests something even older and perhaps even external to Middle-earth, as in 'at the beginning [of time]' or creation of the universe.

A reference in these draft notes to the necromancer - a term used in *The Hobbit* in reference to an early manifestation of Sauron - is also reinforcement of this ageless element, and marks an expansion of the character's connection with the greater legendarium and beyond, prior to the events of the Third Age. A relationship with Farmer Maggot is subject to questioning by Tolkien, as is the link between the Black Riders or Ringwraiths, and the Barrow-wights.

In the final published version, the latter do not circle the house of Bombadil and Goldberry at night as they did in the drafts. Instead, Tolkien merely has Old Man Willow tapping on the window, as happened on the couple's wedding night in the original 1934 verse. This is an interesting note in the fact that it reveals the methodology Tolkien used in developing his text during these early stages and in putting his inner thoughts on paper, with the development of a mixture of possible scenarios, interspersed with personal comments and new content. For example, in an early draft, Tom's answer to the question from Frodo 'Who are you, Master?' is given in terms which he is undoubtedly hopeful the hobbit can understand:

'Eh, what?' said Tom sitting up, and his eyes glinted in the gloom. 'I am an Aborigine, that's what I am, the Aborigine of this land. I have spoken a mort of languages and called myself by many names. Mark my words, my merry friends: Tom was here before the River or the Trees. Tom remembers the first acorn and the first rain-drop. He made paths before the Big People, and saw the Little People arriving. He was here before the kings and the graves and the [ghosts] Barrow-wights. When the Elves passed westward Tom was here already - before the seas were bent. He saw the Sun rise in the West and the Moon following, before the new order of days was made. He knew the dark under the stars when it was fearless - before the Dark Lord came from Outside. (Return of the Shadow)

Within the published version the language of the equivalent paragraph reflects a tighter integration with that of the legendarium. It appears, in part, as follows:

But you are young and I am old. Eldest, that's what I am. Mark my words, my friends: Tom was here before the river and the trees; Tom remembers the first raindrop and the first acorn. He made paths before the Big People, and saw the little People arriving. He was here before the Kings and the graves and the Barrow-wights. When the Elves passed westward, Tom was here already, before the seas were bent. He knew the dark under the stars when it was fearless – before the Dark Lord came from Outside. (LOTR)

These are significant pieces of text, in both draft and final form, as they address the question of who, and perhaps what, Tom is, identifying him as older than the creation of Middle-earth. They also outline some of the historical events he witnessed and point to material that is found in Tolkien's substantially written *The Silmarillion*, which was only published after his death (Tolkien 1977). *The Silmarillion* largely dealt with events outside of, and before, those in the main body of *The Lord of the Rings*, though a few overlapping elements are referred to and included in the latter's published appendices. Tolkien was not successful in having *The Silmarillion* published prior to the release of *The Lord of the Rings*, despite his best efforts. A reading of the two texts clearly reveals why the publisher baulked at issuing the sprawling, complex, and unfinished *Silmarillion* first. However, by writing in this manner, and including inexplicable elements such as a reference to when the world 'was fearless' or 'the Dark Lord came from Outside', the author initially left readers with seemingly unanswerable questions around Tom Bombadil's identity. These mystical and mysterious elements were added to as the drafting progressed.

For example, another early draft introduces the element of Tom's relationship with the Ring of Power. This could have had a significant impact upon the development of the narrative, though whether it was consciously or unconsciously done, as was the author's wont during the drafting process, is unknown. Once introduced, Tolkien chose to develop it to a degree whereby it became an important, though at the same time seemingly offhand, element of Bombadil's characterisation. It is clear that, during this preliminary drafting stage, Tolkien had not fully developed, or identified, the relationship between Tom and the Ring of Power. Neither did he adequately explain within *The Lord of the Rings* the mechanics of the ring's operation and the meaning of the related ability to bring about the disappearance of the wearer when it was worn. This was only revealed in subsequent correspondence, and within texts associated with *The Silmarillion,* though the latter contained no specific reference to Tom Bombadil or his relationship with the Ring of Power. An assessment of the connection between the seeming disappearance of the ring and the planes of reality evident within *The Lord of the Rings* reveals the physical world inhabited by Bombadil and the extra-dimensional wraith-world, with Tom apparently able to manipulate the ring, and himself, between these two planes (Seth 2015). Within the Peter Jackson movies we see Frodo slip between these parallel dimensions whenever he wears the Ring of Power. It is likely that Tom is able to inhabit or experience either space at will, or, as a spirit being he is naturally attuned to both planes.

The draft manuscript was much altered by Tolkien, resulting in a mental strengthening and character development of Tom, Goldberry and the hobbits. We see, for example, that Tom can be melancholy in his memories of the past, to such an extent that he stops talking. It is possible that the brooch he gathers from the Barrow-wight's treasure belonged to a former love of his, thereby highlighting the negative side of an immortal life amongst mortals, and similar to the circumstances facing Aragorn and Arwen. These drafts also suggest that Tom will live through until the end of time, just as he was there at the beginning. He is able to talk about the distant future 'when the world is mended' and the spirits of the departed will return to earth. Immortality is now clearly suggested here.

In the final version there is no encounter with the Black Riders whilst Tom is still with the hobbits. Neither do we see Tom warding them off with a wave of his hand. Yet one draft points to Tom's power at hiding the hobbits. The fact that, within the final published text, the Black Riders do not follow the hobbits into the Old Forest and to Tom's house, is seemingly due to this. He appears to provide a spatial realm in which the thoughts and senses of Sauron's agents are not able to penetrate, thereby masking the hobbits' presence and providing them with a window of opportunity in which to escape, rest and prepare for the journey ahead. The hobbits are also not fearful of the Black Riders while they are with Tom. He had performed a similar duty in protecting the living entities of the Old Forest, and to some degree the Barrow-downs where he resided with Goldberry. It could therefore be suggested that if not for Tom, the Old Forest would not have survived. It also perhaps explains that inexplicable point in the Peter Jackson film where the hobbits hide under a dirt ledge and the Ringwraith above them is not able to sense their immediate presence, despite being mere inches from them and the Ring of Power worn by Frodo.

Within an early draft we see the hobbits, as they leave the Shire and depart from Tom, feeling 'really lonely, exiled and rather helpless' as a group. Yet in the final version only the 'deep loneliness and sense of loss' remains in their leaving Tom and Goldberry behind, for Tolkien enhances the enabling effect of both upon them as they no longer feel helpless (LOTR 144). They have been strengthened for the journey ahead through their time with Tom and Goldberry, and Tom has moved from being a simple earth spirit to something much more powerful and influential (Beal 2018). This is no more evident than in his relationship with the Ring of Power. This use of a ring by Sauron is similar to the devices used by the Voldemort / Tom Riddle character in the *Harry Potter* series and referred to as horcruxes. Therein, elements of one's spirit are dispersed amongst a variety of objects, including within Harry Potter himself (Rowling 2007). As such, and with the ability to make the Ring of Power disappear, Tom is a powerful force in the fight against Sauron, and the latter would likely be aware of this. At one point, in a note written around 1940 and covering a number of chapters from the first book of *The Lord of the Rings*, Tolkien wrote the following:

(2) Tom could have got rid of the Ring all along [without further] .... *If asked!* (The Treason of Isengard)

This extraordinary statement can be interpreted in a number of ways, beyond the obvious pronouncement of Bombadil's power in dealing with Sauron's ring. It can be read as Tolkien realising that the words of Gandalf at the Council of Elrond had stopped that body from making use of Tom Bombadil to destroy the Ring of Power, or at least remove it from the influence of Sauron. It could also represent Tolkien's identification of a flaw in the narrative when Tom briefly makes it disappear. Or, as is most likely, this is a meaningful element of the narrative, and considered and reinforced as such by Tolkien. Of course, if this scenario had been developed and Tom been given responsibility for dealing with the Ring of Power, the quest would have come to a swift end. The same may have happened if the eagles of Manwë had flown the hobbits from the Shire to Mordor, instead of merely rescuing them from the fires of Mount Doom – a scenario which has been postulated on numerous fan websites. It is therefore both surprising and revealing that Tolkien should make such a comment and was mindful of the possible scenario. Nevertheless, he left the Ring of Power disappearance element in the published version, no doubt to highlight the fact that there is usually an alternative to pursuing the path of war, even if that alternative does not serve every need. It also explained the representation of the 'certain things otherwise left out' sentiment later expressed by the author in regards to Tom's role.

Tom Bombadil, the powerful pacifist, played no active role in the Fellowship of the Ring as a result of the statements made, and arguments put, at the Council of Elrond. The 'war room' (Council of Elrond) and 'the generals' (Elrond, Gandalf, etc.) overrode common sense and compassion, as Tolkien himself experienced in the actions of the British generals during World War I and upon the battlefields of France by those in command, resulting in the extension of a war in which many lives were needlessly lost on both sides before 'victory', or resolution, was attained.

Tolkien's unpublished drafts and published worlds reveal that whoever and whatever Tom Bombadil is - for the *who* and the *what* are not the same - he is not simply 'Tom Bombadil'. That is merely one of many labels used at a specific time and place in the history of Middle-earth, and by specific individuals or groups. He is, as he himself says, both eldest and Eldest. To the hobbits of the Shire, he is Tom Bombadil – a name apparently given him by the people of Buckland, 'to add to his many other ones' (Tolkien 1962, Preface). To the Elves he is known as Iarwain Ben-adar (translated as eldest, energetic and fatherless) and Yare's (reminiscent of the Hebrew word Yahweh, meaning God); the Dwarves call him Forn; to the Gnomes he is Erion; the Northern Men use Orald (a variant on old); and to some, including Frodo, he is simply the Master. We see a plethora of names, with each having arisen over an extensive period of time and under different circumstances. Tolkien enjoyed giving his characters multiple names, and perhaps none more so than Tom Bombadil.

Gandalf the Grey was a Maiar or wizard, a spirit created to assist the Valar in shaping Arda. Following his death and transformation into Gandalf the White, he was placed on a closer footing to Tom Bombadil and better able to fulfil the need to communicate with him. Prior to this he was both ignorant and seemingly intimidated by him, and this may have given rise to the comments at the Council of Elrond where Tom is portrayed by Gandalf and others as useless in the war against Sauron and Saruman, and, in part, as a selfish buffoon similar to Shakespeare's Poor Tom. In fact, he was none of these, and Gandalf the White was obviously very much aware of this and perhaps of the role Bombadil had played in emboldening the hobbits.

Upon publication of the first volume of *The Lord of the Rings* in 1954, Tolkien was met with a flurry of correspondence from those wishing to discuss aspects of his work. The issue of Tom Bombadil featured amongst the many requests for further information, and these continued throughout his lifetime. Within that private correspondence, the author almost immediately made a number of significant statements in regards to Tom, including providing tantalising hints as to his true nature, beyond what was revealed within the published work. In some of the correspondence it is as though Tolkien is commenting upon another author's work, for there is a distance in the perspective and apparent revelations as to the possible implications of what has been written. For example, on 25 February 1954, in a letter to proof reader Naomi Mitchison, Tolkien commented at length on aspects of the character:

... I think it is good that there should be a lot of things unexplained (especially if an explanation actually exists) ... And even in a mythical Age there must be some enigmas, as there always are. Tom Bombadil is one (intentionally)..... Tom Bombadil is not an important person – to the narrative. I suppose he has some importance as a 'comment'. I mean, I do not really write like that: he is just an invention (who first appeared in the Oxford Magazine about 1933 [1934]), and he represents something that I feel important, though I would not be prepared to analyze the feeling precisely. I would not, however, have left him in, if he did not have some kind of function. I might put it this way. The story is cast in terms of a good side, and a bad side, beauty against ruthless ugliness, tyranny against kingship, moderated freedom with

consent against compulsion that has long lost any object save mere power, and so on; but both sides in some degree, conservative or destructive, want a measure of control. But if you have, as it were, taken 'a vow of poverty', renounced control, and take your delight in things for themselves without reference to yourself, watching, observing, and to some extent knowing, then the question of the rights and wrongs of power and control might become utterly meaningless to you, and the means of power quite valueless. It is a natural pacifist view, which arises in the mind when there is a war. But the view in Rivendell seems to be that it is an excellent thing to have represented, but that there are in fact things with which it cannot cope; and upon which its existence nonetheless depends. Ultimately only the victory of the West will allow Bombadil to continue, or even to survive. Nothing would be left for him in the world of Sauron.... (*Letters* 144)

Herein, Tolkien raises the notion of Tom as an enigma, though as ever equivocating in regards to the precise role he played in the creation of the character. His final two sentences refer to the view at the Council of Elrond, that Bombadil was like them and susceptible to the will and power of Sauron, and that only their actions could save him and the rest of Middle-earth. Of course, Tom Bombadil was not like them at all, and their premise was false. The letter contains some of Tolkien's deepest reflections on the character of Tom Bombadil and his own philosophical view of war and peace. Tolkien recognised the need to fight for peace, especially against foes such as the Nazis under Adolf Hitler. But he also believed in, and supported, the need to resist the idea of war at all cost whilst at the same time providing alms and advice in order to achieve this. Tom Bombadil is such a person – a pacifist, an anti-war 'hippie' to put him in a more modern context, but a powerful ally and a reflection of what Tolkien had become following his horrific experiences in World War I. In addition, the comment is guarded and perhaps somewhat disingenuous, couched in vagaries and suppositions which raise questions rather than provide clarity – though we must consider the possibility that Tolkien was meaningfully being obstructive, or genuinely lacked clarity about the character and what he had written. Nevertheless, he is making Bombadil enigmatic by enriching the characterisation but omitting vital background detail. Or is he?

We must / should / can assume Tolkien knows who and what Tom is when he states that 'he represents something that I feel important', but he is not prepared to tell us what or why, or even take himself down a path that he himself had seemingly travelled, and had engaged with since writing that initial draft some seventeen years previous. Tom indeed represents the 'natural pacifist view' which seeks peace, love and compassion, yet Tolkien's Middle-earth at that point in time required, and represented, a world of generals and armies continuously striving for the 'victory of the West' in order to secure that peace.

Numerous clues as to Tom's true nature and the context in which he was developed are provided to the reader in the aforementioned letters, draft manuscripts and published text. For example, Tolkien's experience of war, both in the trenches of the Western Front during World War I and as an active observer and parent during World War II, gives rise to his intimate awareness of that so-called 'pacifist view' which is actually part of the normal, everyday way of life both during times of war and beyond. It is also related, in his specific instance, to leading a good, Christian life. Tolkien's comments, and by implication the actions of Tom Bombadil, in turn reflect a Buddhist perspective, highlighting mindfulness and a rejection of the individual quest for power and the suffering that engenders. He also outlines his view regarding that pursued by the seat of power, which in this case is Rivendell and the Council of Elrond. In subsequent correspondence, Tolkien would maintain this enigmatic stance regarding Bombadil and, by association, Goldberry. For example, on 21 August 1954, shortly after publication of *The Fellowship of the Ring*, the first book of *The Lord of the Rings*, Tolkien wrote to Nevill Coghill in regards to the inexplicable, though also expansive nature of Tom Bombadil, and his possible vulnerability:

But Tom Bombadil is just as he is. Just an odd 'fact' of that world. He won't be explained, because as long as you are (as in this tale you are meant to be) concentrated on the Ring, he is inexplicable. But he's there – a reminder of the truth (as I see it) that the world is so large and manifold that if you take one facet and fix your mind and heart on it, there is always something that does not come in to that story / argument / approach, and seems to belong to a larger story. But of course, in another way, not that of pure story-making, Bombadil is a deliberate contrast to the Elves who are artists. But B. does not want to make, alter, devise, or control anything: just to observe and take joy in the contemplating the things that are not himself. The spirit of the [deleted: world > this earth] made aware of itself. He is more like science (utterly free from technological blemish) and history than art. He represents the complete fearlessness of that spirit when we can catch a little of it. But I do suggest that it is possible to fear (as I do) that the making artistic sub-creative spirit (of Men and Elves) is actually more potent, and can 'fall', and that it could in the eventual triumph of its own evil destroy the whole earth, and Bombadil and all. (Hammond and Scull 2018)

This letter once again outlines the complex philosophical underpinnings of the character and his place within the overall narrative, presenting Bombadil as real and significant, belonging to 'a larger story' and a beacon of hope in a world which may ultimately destroy itself. Tolkien tells us quite forcefully that in our efforts to understand him we should - nay, must - look away from the ring quest and consider that bigger picture. 'He won't be explained,' he tells us. This has been at the core of the Tom Bombadil problem in that his character, whilst an important and integral part of the hobbits' world, is not part of the core *The Lord of the Rings* narrative. It belongs beyond that, extending into the realm of *The Silmarillion*.

Tolkien followed the Coghill letter up with another during September 1954. In a surviving draft response to Peter Hastings, proprietor of a Catholic bookshop, the author addresses references in the book to Tom as 'the Master' and the proposition, as Hastings sees it, that Bombadil is a manifestation of God on Middle-earth. Tolkien's response is, as within the previous two letters, both evasive, as he never actually denies Hastings' assertion, and expansively informative:

...As for Tom Bombadil, I really do think you are being too serious, besides missing the point. (Again, the words used are by Goldberry and Tom, not me as a commentator). You rather remind me of a Protestant relation who to me objected to the (modern) Catholic habit of calling priests Father, because the name father belonged only to the First Person, citing last Sunday's Epistle - inappositely since that says ex quo. Lots of other characters are called Master; and if 'in time' Tom was primeval he was Eldest in Time. But Goldberry and Tom are referring to the mystery of names. See and ponder Tom's words in Vol. I p. 142 [I.7:129]. You may be able to conceive of your unique relation to the Creator without a name - can you? For in such a relation pronouns become proper nouns. But as soon as you are in a world of other finites with a similar, if each unique and different, relation to [the] Prime Being, who are

*you? Frodo has asked not 'what is Tom Bombadil' but 'Who is he'. We and he no doubt laxly confuse the questions. Goldberry gives what I think is the correct answer. We need not go into the sublimities of 'I am that I am' - which is quite different from 'he is'. * [*Only the first person (of worlds or anything) can be unique. If you say 'he is' there must be more than one, and created (sub) existence is implied. I can say 'he is' of Winston Churchill as well as of Tom Bombadil, surely?] She adds as a concession a statement of part of the 'what'. He is master in a peculiar way: he has no fear, and no desire of possession or domination at all. He merely knows and understands about such things as concern him in his natural little realm. He hardly even judges, and as far as can be seen makes no effort to reform or remove even the Willow. I don't think Tom needs philosophizing about, and is not improved by it. But many have found him an odd or indeed discordant ingredient. In historical fact I put him in because I had already 'invented' him independently (he first appeared in the Oxford Magazine) and wanted an 'adventure' on the way. But I kept him in, and as he was, because he represents certain things otherwise left out. I do not mean him to be an allegory - or I should not have given him so particular, individual, and ridiculous a name - but 'allegory' is the only mode of exhibiting certain functions: he is then an 'allegory', or an exemplar, a particular embodying of pure (real) natural science: the spirit that desires knowledge of other things, their history and nature, because they are 'other' and wholly independent of the enquiring mind, a spirit coeval with the* *rational mind, and entirely unconcerned with 'doing' anything with the knowledge: Zoology and Botany not Cattle-breeding or Agriculture. Even the Elves hardly show this: they are primarily artists. Also T.B. exhibits another point in his attitude to the Ring, and its failure to affect him. You must concentrate on some part, probably relatively small, of the World (Universe), whether to tell a tale, however long, or to learn anything, however fundamental — and therefore much will from that 'point of view' be left out, distorted on the circumference, or seem a discordant oddity. The power of the Ring over all concerned, even the Wizards or Emissaries, is not a delusion — but it is not the whole picture, even of the then state and content of that part of the Universe....* (Letter 153)

This letter, though cryptic in many ways, is perhaps ultimately the most revelatory in regards to both who and what Tom Bombadil is. In it Tolkien admits to the character's allegorical credentials and to being both a 'particular embodying' and 'a spirit', but does not openly reveal any hidden religious meaning, apart from Tom being a goodly pacifist as against an evil warmonger. He then informs us that if he had meant Bombadil to be an allegory he would have given him a special name, as he did with many other beings through the use of Quenya, a fictional language devised by Tolkien around 1913 and purportedly used by the Elves. Tolkien is playing games here, as he actually did give him such a name, as in the Elvish Iarwain Ben-adar. But Tom Bombadil was already in play.

Perhaps one of his children had originated the name and it therefore took precedence. The fact that Tom possessed a 'ridiculous' name derived from a toy did not, nevertheless, hinder development of the character.

Tolkien's defensiveness is limited, due to the fact that he allowed Goldberry to let the cat out of the bag, so to speak, when she informed Frodo that Tom was master of 'wood, water and hill', which refers not only to Middle-earth, but to the world generally, called by Tolkien Arda, and to its creation. What such mastery entails is not made clear. Is he God, the creator, called by Tolkien Eru? This relates to the questions of 'what' Tom is. We know 'who' he is from his actions within the book and statements by those who knew him, or knew of him. But we are not sure 'what' he is i.e., what kind of being he is, or his true nature, apart from Goldberry's partial answer in referring to him rather vaguely as 'the Master'.

Perhaps of most significance is the fact that Tolkien points out in the Hastings letter that you don't need a name in order to consider a relationship with the Creator – the 'Prime Being' - which in this particular instance is seemingly referring to Tom Bombadil and the initial question by Hastings as to whether he was a representation of God. A name is not important in this specific instance. In discussing the numerous names allocated to Bombadil, Tolkien points to 'the Creator without a name.' This follows on Tom's own rejection of the idea of a name, merely telling Frodo that he is

'Eldest' and therefore, in fact, nameless, i.e., he is the nameless Creator. The absence of a name is therefore linked to the Creator or Prime Being, which is of course a matter of supreme significance to Tolkien, who made language and names the very foundation of his greater legendarium. As such, the common reading of this letter as a refutation of the claim that Tom is a manifestation of God is shown to be false, as Tolkien does not openly reject the proposition. In fact, he deflects a straight Yes / No answer by belittling his correspondent as being 'too serious' and then providing a cryptic answer which seems, on the surface, to support the assertion. Furthermore, Tolkien's statement: '*If you say 'he is' there must be more than one, and created (sub) existence is implied,*' makes sense in the context of the Christian concept of the Blessed Trinity to which Tolkien adhered (Williams 2003, Hensler 2013, Tolkien Fans 2013, Moxon 2014, Klamut n.d.). A more expansive discussion of this aspect of the characterisation of Tom Bombadil is included below, though the Hastings letter remains core to the revelation of the Godliness of Tom Bombadil.

Tolkien extols the importance of the character whilst skirting around the question of what Tom Bombadil is, though nevertheless offering clues. The letter and 'fatherless' comment would suggest that Tom's origin is beyond the point of creation, for the world described in *The Lord of the Rings* is intimately connected with that outlined in *The Silmarillion*, and it is within this latter published, though substantially earlier written work that the origin of the universe is revealed. This letter provides part of the reason for the author's subterfuge around Bombadil's true identity, in that he 'does not fit [within Middle-earth] and opens as it were a window into some other system'. What that other system precisely is Tolkien was not prepared to reveal, or elaborate upon at that point, but would leave up to the reader to discover, whilst providing hints along the way.

CHAPTER 4:

Deliberate Discordance and the Power of Tom

F rom Tom Bombadil's first appearance in *The Lord of the Rings* there has been vigorous discussion and debate around precisely who and what he is, and why Tolkien included him in the famous work despite the fact that he was such 'an odd or indeed discordant ingredient' (Letter 153). The inclusion was, in part, explained in the aforementioned correspondence commencing from 1954, the year in which *The Fellowship of the Ring* was first published. Therein Tolkien indicated he included Bombadil because he was already written and therefore an easy addition as he set to the task of writing a sequel to *The Hobbit.* Tom also provided adventure on the way, to both Tolkien and the reader. As the book developed there was a need to retain the character, but he did not feel an obligation or desire to ultimately expand upon the descriptions given, though he did alter Bombadil's essence, dramatically expanding it. He also cryptically noted that Tom Bombadil was important, though not necessarily to the narrative – a conclusion readers and adaptors such as film directors Ralph Bakshi and Peter Jackson would also reach.

Information about 'who' Tom is was supplied both within the text and subsequent correspondence; information regarding 'what' Tom is was not. One likely reason for this stance on the part of Tolkien was that, due to Tom's inherent allegorical nature, a more expansive explanation of his origins could have resulted in accusations of allegory being levelled against the book as a whole. This was something the author did not want. Tom was an allegorical figure, much like the autobiographical Niggle in *Leaf by Niggle* (Tolkien 1945). However, the public was not to necessarily know about, or focus, on this, despite the many clues the author left behind. They were meant to focus on the hobbits' quest. In addition, Tolkien would not encourage the search for hidden meaning within the character, as that would open up a veritable can of worms. Later prose references to Bombadil, such as 1962's *Bombadil Goes Boating*, did not address the issue of what the character was, being merely descriptive of events and harking back to the character's late 1920s juvenile and extra-legendarium origins. Bombadil therefore remained the enigma as portrayed in *The Lord of the Rings*. Despite the fact that during his lifetime Tolkien wrote a lot about him, he never wrote enough to satisfy the fans and critics, keeping Tom's true nature elusive, at least on the surface, to the end. Tolkien provided no backstory or community of Bombadils, as he had done for Middle-earth sentient species such as hobbits, dwarves, elves, men and ents. Perhaps this was because, for some reason, there could not be such things, and Tom was, indeed, a singular entity. Is there, nevertheless, a way to better understand him and solve a seemingly unsolvable mystery?

A study of extant manuscripts and beyond what is commonly gleaned through a reading of *The Lord of the Rings*, reveals that Tom Bombadil is a significant character both in and of himself, and also in regards to the quest to destroy the Ring of Power. It is the former that is of most interest here, and which leads us to consider his true nature, rather than the more commonly discussed quest to defeat Sauron. Firstly, there are a number of reasons why Bombadil is important to both *The Lord of the Rings* and the wider Tolkien cosmology, beyond simply providing 'adventure on the way'. These include the fact that he protects the hobbits from the pursuing Black Riders / Ringwraiths; he saves them from Old Man Willow of the Old Forest, and from the Barrow-wights of the Barrow Downs; he and Goldberry rejuvenate the hobbits in their house, reviving their strength through rest, food, words and song; Bombadil provides them with swords that will assist in their quest; he strengthens their spirits for the task ahead, through his actions, teachings and positive outlook; he provides the lead hobbit Frodo Baggins with prophecy which enables him to understand his ultimate goal of reaching 'a far green country' (Letter 91, Greenie

2003); he shows the hobbits that there are things of import other than the quest to destroy the Ring of Power; and he is a protector of the Old Forest and all living entities within it, including Old Man Willow and his own partner Goldberry. All told, Bombadil offers much of import to the hobbits and their quest to destroy the Ring of Power.

The hobbits' time with Tom can be likened to the training required by soldiers as a prelude to war, similar to Tolkien's own training in association with World War I. Bombadil's boot camp gears them up for the task ahead, though not in an overtly physical way. He does, however, upon their first meeting, force them to run along a path by the Withywindle River towards his house, with no quarter given to their small stature and weariness. This is despite the fact that by the previous day they had already become exhausted. In this role Bombadil is the powerful and positive pacifist. It may therefore appear that nothing much happens in regards to the flow of *The Lord of the Rings* narrative whilst the hobbits are with Tom and Goldberry, and this has been stated by a number of commentators. However, if not for Bombadil's intervention at this early stage, the quest would likely end sooner, either within the strangling and revengeful roots of Old Man Willow; on a cold, concrete slab in a Barrow-wight cavern, with their bodies bejewelled, breathless and soulless; or on the road to Bree at the hands of the Black Riders. Tom and Goldberry are important to *The Lord of the Rings* both for what they do and what they represent. It is true that they could have been left out of the story and the hobbits' journey from the Shire to Bree may have proceeded without incident or adventure, largely as it is depicted in audio and on film. But this is not how the book was written, and to ignore Bombadil and Goldberry is to do a disservice to the author and the integrity of his work. It is also to omit vital elements of the real and imaginary world as Tolkien saw it. Tom can be said to represent Plato's moral person, who rejects power, preferring 'to live a life of inner peace and integrity' (Katz 2003). He and Goldberry appear to share an idyll of happiness, like Adam and Eve in a veritable Garden of Eden. As one commentator has suggested:

That Frodo's eastward journey is delayed is no blunder of narrative construction, for it is just the kind of happiness encapsulated in this episode, the happiness of grateful contemplation of beauty, of unforced, unhurried activity, practical and creative, which the work opposes to the nihilistic spirit of Mordor. We need to feel its allure, not only in order to sustain our interest in the fulfilment of Frodo's mission, but also because the imagining of such happiness (which like any object of desire is most compelling when transient or imperilled) is central to the purpose of The Lord of the Rings. (Rosebury 2001)

The bliss of Bombadil and Goldberry domesticity's, combined with memories of the Shire, provide the hobbits with motivation to complete their journey and find ultimate peace at home or elsewhere, such as within the Undying Lands to which Bilbo and Frodo ultimately travel. Within the Peter Jackson films this bliss is derived solely from life in the Shire, as in Sam's dreams of marriage and Frodo's joy at his place within the community. The excision of the idyllic life of Tom Bombadil and Goldberry from filmic and other versions of *The Lord of the Rings* detracts not only from the richness of the original story telling, but also results in the loss of a pacifist view in a tale of war, and the presence of a powerful female figure, as in a goddess, within a world of men.

Tolkien stated in 1937 that Bombadil was perhaps 'fully enshrined' in the 1934 verse *The Adventures of Tom Bombadil* (Letter 19). However, he then went on to substantially expand the character in association with the writing of *The Lord of the Rings*. Upon publication of that expansive work, it was understandable that readers wanted to know more about him, for they were not privy to any background information concerning Tolkien's conscious or subconscious thoughts during the drafting process. Nor was the content of *The Silmarillion*, and the complex, almost encyclopaedic context it provided to the events of the Third Age seen in *The Lord of the Rings*, generally accessible to readers prior to 1977. Tolkien accommodated readers and reviewers to a very limited degree within his personal correspondence, but once again much of that was not made public until 1981, with the publication of an edited collection (Tolkien 1981). Neither did the three additional prose pieces including Tom provide answers. Bombadil therefore remained a mystery to contemporary and later audiences, both within and without *The Lord of the Rings*. Tolkien nevertheless provides us with clues to, supposedly, unravel the mystery as to who Tom is.

In pointing to his own longevity, Tom speaks in the third person, telling us how 'Tom was here... He was here.....' He also sings of himself 'Ho! Tom Bombadil!' However, nobody in *The Lord of the Rings* addresses him by the simple, personal Tom. Within the drafting of the book Tolkien eventually deleted references to close relations with Barnabas Butterbur, the innkeeper at Bree, with Farmer Maggot, with Aragorn, and even with Gandalf, leaving Bombadil somewhat isolated, apart from his intimate relationship with Goldberry, the being most closely related to him in form and spirit nature. Goldberry appears to be related to, or reflective of, Tom Bombadil beyond being his wife, in presenting as the human form of an earth-bound spirit. The two therefore maintain a connection both as partners and within the spiritual realm as embodiments of particular elements of nature. For Tom it is a generalised 'earth' or Arda; for Goldberry it is water: she is the daughter of the river. In is notable that in the Catholic pantheon the Virgin Mary is closely associated with water. Upon the hobbits' first encountering Goldberry, she is seated and we learn that:

...about her feet in wide vessels of green and brown earthenware, white water-lilies were floating, so that she seems to be enthroned in the midst of a pool. (LOTR)

Tom's securing of the last water lilies of the season was an obvious sign of his attachment to Goldberry, and the point at which he supposedly came across the hobbits by chance, though he later tells them that he knew they were coming. In both instances Tolkien has made the two characters both corporeal and spirit. This narrative isolation is the main reason for omission from adaptations of the book, and is reinforced by the veil of mystery hanging over their identities, and most especially Tom's.

Frodo calls Tom's name in song when trapped by the Barrow-wights, and later refers to 'old Bombadil'. Likewise, Goldberry's statement that 'He is' could be interpreted as telling us that, despite any persona given him by those in Middle-earth, Tom basically is who he is and does not need a name, though she also goes on to seemingly complete the sentence with the equally mysterious statement that 'He is the Master.' Master of what, and/or whom? As to Tom's identity, to a query from Frodo, he answers: 'Don't you know my name yet? That is the only answer.' In other words, he is, at that point, just a meaningless name - Tom Bombadil - and beyond that there is nothing else, apart from what people perceive or experience in their encounters with him. There is no lineage, no revelation, no explanation that the author is prepared to give to the hobbits, or the readers. Such a mysterious, metaphysical being is unique to Middle-earth and for this reason has, to date, defied identification or classification. The question must therefore be asked: Why has Tolkien intentionally presented us with a significant, though enigmatic being and then suggested that we should not look deeper, or philosophise over his origins? Did the Tom Bombadil of *The Lord of the Rings* autonomously rise out of the ether during the writing process? Was Tolkien truly unaware of his origins, in whole or part? The latter is not such a strange proposition, for Clyde Kilby, an American author and professor of English at Wheaton College who worked with Tolkien during 1966 on initial editing of *The Silmarillion*, noted the following:

[Tolkien] was also aware of an even deeper meaning and origin of his fiction. He said that a member of parliament had stood in the room we were in and declared "<u>You</u> did not write the Lord of the Rings," meaning it had been given him from God. It was clear that he favoured this remark. (Kilby 1976)

Such a suggestion is not contrary to the position the author subsequently took, for Tolkien, in defending the book, informed us that Tom Bombadil is necessary, important and real, in both a physical and spiritual sense. He is therefore obviously the product of Tolkien's conscious and unconscious thought processes. This can also help explain why the author refused to explain what he was, or allocate him a place in the Middle-earth legendarium as detailed and as complex as individuals such as, for example, Gandalf, Elrond, Galadriel and Sauron. Kilby actually pressed Tolkien during 1966 to implant Bombadil within *The Silmarillion* and the First Age of the greater legendarium, but the author, by then 74 years old and occupied with issues such as the ailing health of his beloved Edith, never got around to doing that. As a result, on the surface it would appear that he was simply dropped into *The Lord of the Rings* and then abandoned by the author, with only slight modifications from the original 1934 verse. But such is not the case.

Incongruous, discordant, enigmatic, mysterious – all labels that can be applied to Tom Bombadil, and all behind his historic exclusion from film and other public presentations of *The Lord of the Rings*. A deeper understanding of both the character and the author suggests that there was a reason why Tom Bombadil remained as written, and hidden. However, in lieu of Tolkien's reticence to reveal all, Bombadil has been identified as many things by many people, just as he was in Middle-earth at the end of the Third Age. This is due in part to an active fan base and, within that, an often understandably limited awareness of Tolkien's complex mythology and the forces behind its creation and evolution. Arguments around what Tom Bombadil is invariably contain elements of truth, though none fully explain his place in Middle-earth, or even his role in the quest to destroy Sauron's ring. A reading of the aforementioned outline of the character's development through *The Lord of the Rings* drafting process reveals a pastiche of both the conscious and unconscious thoughts and beliefs of the author as sub-creator. The portrait of Tom presented in the final, published version adds considerably to this, refined over the years 1939-48 following on its initial drafting between late 1937 and the middle of 1938. Tolkien obviously made many changes and refinements during that latter decade. As a result, we see that Bombadil is a being who, in part like Gandalf, is imbued with special powers, but at the same time, and unlike Gandalf, is unique amongst the inhabitants of Middle-earth. Neither does he fit neatly into the hierarchy of beings revealed within *The Silmarillion,* though some commentators have attempted to do this. The display of special powers in large part gives rise to the enigmatic nature of his character. Tom Bombadil is no ordinary being, possessing as he does, for example, an affinity with natural objects such as trees, which are the traditional symbols of divine knowledge, alongside water spirits and animals. We observe in Bombadil elements of an earth spirit, but beyond that, and from the world of *The Silmarillion*, also hierarchical entities such as Eru (God), the Valar, Maiar and even angelic Ainur, many of whom are, on the surface, foreign to *The Lord of the Rings*. Gandalf is a Maiar, as is Radagast the Brown, whose affinity with animals is on display in Jackson's *The Hobbit* trilogy (2012-14). Tom's powers and attributes, nevertheless, are wide ranging and can be seen to include the following:

· *Hypnotic*: Tom is able to induce sleep deeper than a hypnotic trance in living entities, through words, song and thoughts. This is first seen in 1934's *The Adventures of Tom Bombadil*, wherein Tom puts to sleep, in turn, Old Man Willow, a family of badgers, a ghostly Barrow-wight, and Goldberry, a river spirit. Within *The*

Lord of the Rings he likewise induces sleep in Old Man Willow ('Go to sleep') and the four hobbits – Frodo, Sam, Merry and Pippin.

· *Power of thought*: Tom is able to ward off the Barrow-wights who have entrapped the hobbits, through his spoken words, unspoken thoughts, action and the use of light. He can also stop living entities from moving, as though they are frozen and trapped. For example, his distant words and songs 'enchant' the hobbits and halt them in their tracks before they first meet. He then says to Frodo and Sam, 'Whoa! Steady there!' and they stop 'as if they had been struck stiff.' Tom's words alone stop the Old Man Willow from further constricting Merry and Pippin, and generating movement amongst the surrounding trees, even before Tom is in sight. He then sings to Old Man Willow 'Poor old Willow-man, you tuck your roots away!' in order for them to be released.

· *Projection*: Tom is able to project his words, songs and thoughts through space, such that those at a distance are affected. Likewise, he is able to perceive thoughts and feelings, as in when Frodo sings a specific plea for help from deep within the Barrow-wight cavern and Tom immediately answers the call from afar, appearing almost instantaneously. This is evidence of Bombadil's spiritual nature and the fact that he is not simply earthbound, but operates in a multi-dimensional plane. No explanation for this ability is provided by the author.

· *Protection*: The fact that the hobbits are not discovered by Sauron and the Ringwraiths whilst with Tom, appears due to his power to mask their presence and thereby protect all those who inhabit the Old Forest. This power may go further in 'scaring off' evil forces from entering a space which is protected by him. Perhaps Goldberry also wields this power. There is no explanation for this apart from the fact of it occurring. During the Council of Elrond this seemingly localised power of protection in regard to the Old Forest is noted as a disadvantage to Tom's usefulness therein, with the members failing to see the possible universality of its application.

· *Immortality*: Tom is eldest and ancient, with an immortality which appears to go beyond that experienced by the Elves. In his letter to Rhona Beare, Tolkien had pointed out that the "counterfeit" immortality of the Elves, and that sought by Sauron through the ring, was lesser, and that, *True immortality is beyond Eä* (Letter 211). We are told that he was there at the beginning of time and will be there at the end. Though this is not a power as such, it is nevertheless a powerful element of his character, associated with wisdom, knowledge and fearlessness. Immortality is elsewhere equated with invincibility, an absence of vulnerability and strength. Conjecture by Gandalf and others that Bombadil would fail before the might of Sauron are therefore likely erroneous and a misreading of what Tolkien actually said, or implied, in regards to his ultimate fate.

· *Energising:* Tom is able to reverse the process of sleep inducement and, in addition, revive both the body and spirit. This is seen when the hobbits arrive in his house, weary and fearful, only to leave two days later refreshed and emboldened, though much more aware of the difficult task ahead. Goldberry also plays a part here, dispensing positive energy, most obviously in the form of the bright light which surrounds her, similar, in part, to the holy halo which traditionally adorns Catholic figures such as Jesus Christ and the Virgin Mary. We also see this later when Tom rescues the hobbits from captivity in a Barrow cavern, reviving three from near-death states, or possibly death itself. Tolkien makes use of coloured light to reflect the spiritual aspect of this revival. For example, when the hobbits arrive at Bombadil's house, they, along with Goldberry, are bathed in a warm, yellow glow which is representative of a revitalising positive energy. When they hear Tom's song 'Hey come merry dol!' their spirits lift and energy returns (Forest-Hill 2015). Within the Barrow cavern the pale green light of the Barrow-wights saps their spirit and energy, moving them towards death, or perhaps even bringing it upon their cold, lifeless bodies. Tom brings light to the cavern, both saving the hobbits and dispersing the Barrow-wights.

· *Creative power:* Tom has the power of creation, through song and words. He tells Frodo that he must leave the hobbits to their journey and return to 'my making and my singing.' This ability to create is referred to by Tolkien in *The Silmarillion* as a continuation of the work of Eru and the Ainur at the beginning of time, wherein was created the universe Eä out of the Void through the the Flame Imperishable, or Secret Fire. Tom's power to create through words and song is related to his ability to revive, both physically and spiritually, though the extent of this is not made clear. We are told in *The Silmarillion* that only Eru has the power of creation in regard to living, sentient beings. As one online correspondent notes in a discussion on aspects of the Music of the Ainur:

The idea expressed in the Music [of the Ainur], that the most beautiful theme draws much of its power from sorrow, is a theme that underlies virtually all of Tolkien's work, and in my opinion, it is this underlying sorrow that, fittingly, gives his work much of its power. It's a rare work that exemplifies its own theme so perfectly (Cook 2017b).

The eternal joy and melancholic sorrow of Tom Bombadil are powerful elements of his being, reflecting back to this binary element of the Music of the Ainur, the creative force of Tolkien's all-encompassing legendarium.

· *Songs:* Tom's primary means of communication and action is through song and rhythmic verse. He mentions that he has specific songs for specific beings and purposes. For example, he says of Old Man Willow, 'I have a tune for him', which can then be used to make him do as Tom demands. This ability can manifest in a number of different forms, with the words of his songs powerful in and of themselves. Tom's music can cast spells, travel over long distances through space and effect change. The emphasis on song (sound) as a method of creation and empowerment harks back to the creation stories of *The Silmarillion* and the music of Eru and the Ainur. The presence of this ability is an example of what Tolkien refers to as 'a window into some other system' which, in this case, is 'Outside' of the world of Middle-earth and not described, as such, within the main text of *The Lord of the Rings*. Tolkien has allowed himself to drift into this world in regard to the development of the Tom Bombadil character, but has not openly proclaimed the fact.

· *Speed*: Tom is presented in *The Lord of the Rings* as an old man, yet therein descriptions are given as to his 'hopping and dancing', 'leaping on the hill-tops', how he 'bounds', and that 'he ran' faster than the hobbits could run along the Withywindle River to his house. He seems energetic and able to move very fast, beyond what is considered normal for a person of his supposed age. Goldberry also runs. The fact that he reaches the trapped hobbits within the Barrow cavern in a 'long moment' (i.e. almost instantaneously) following Frodo's plaintive song of distress and call for help, suggests that he can actually travel through space in an instant, if needed. This seems to be the reflection of his spirit nature – an element of Faërie, or magic, which Tolkien believes is core to both story-telling and reality (Helms 1974 & 1981, Tolkien 2008). This aspect is underplayed in *The Lord of the Rings*, though it is nevertheless presented to the reader by the author, especially in the character of Tom Bombadil, and more commonly by Gandalf and Galadriel.

· *Power over elements of nature*: Tom threatens Old Man Willow that he will 'freeze his marrow … sing his roots off … sing a wind up and blow leaf and branch away.' This destructive power is not made use of within *The Lord of the Rings*, but Old Man Willow has no qualms in taking it to heart and reacting accordingly, fearful of its application. Tom, apparently, does not have power over the weather, but he can raise or abate the wind and induce cold all the same. In a similar vein Goldberry can make it rain with song, with both working together to turn the weather around so that the hobbits are forced to stay with them an extra day. Tom also sings 'Down west sinks the sun' and Tolkien writes that 'almost at once the sun seemed to sink into the trees behind' the hobbits. Is Tolkien implying that Tom actually makes the sun set? This coincidence points to the intimate relationship between what Tom says or feels and the actions of the earth around him. According to one writer, Tom is the embodiment of nature and the original pure creation of Arda (Frances 2003). However, at the end of the Third Age he appears to be geographically restricted, perhaps due to the encroachment of the forces of evil under Sauron, maintaining a protective attachment to what remains of the Old Forest. The trees therein, such as Old Man Willow, are revengeful (an act of free will), due to destructive deforestation and recent encroachment by, for example, the hobbits of the Shire. The trees may be bitter and twisted, but they are not Sauron's agents of evil, as Tolkien pointed out in his correspondence with Molly Waldron during 1955. Neither does Tom reflect anger or a revengeful nature. His presence next to the Old Forest and close by the Shire could be seen as a planned action following on aeons of travel, in order to be of assistance when the war of the ring commences. In other words, he is in the right place and the right time.

· *Power over Sauron's ring*: Tom is unaffected by the power of the ring and is able to make it disappear. At one point in drafting *The Lord of the Rings*, Tolkien wrote a note stating that Tom could have taken the ring and destroyed it. Gandalf argued the contrary at the Council of Elrond, suggesting that Tom did not have power over the ring and neither could he destroy it, but rather it had no power over him, and therefore he could not serve as ring bearer. If Tom had been given the ring, and indeed destroyed it, Sauron would have been defeated, the hobbits would have returned home and the quest ended. We can also speculate as to what would have been the outcome if Tom had merely made it disappear, or if he and Sauron had met and clashed over its possession. Sauron is a corrupted Maia, similar to Gandalf. Tom is a powerful, enigmatic figure of apparently unknown origin beneath the jolly blue persona. It should not be assumed, therefore, that he is lesser than Sauron, despite Tolkien planting such seeds through the words of

Gandalf and others. Tolkien never directly states that Sauron would defeat Tom, though it is suggested by others. There are obvious limits to Bombadil's power within the context of Arda and Middle-earth, either natural or self-imposed. However, Tom also appears to have a deep connection with the spirit realm, and the Ring of Power is one gateway into that realm. When it is worn, or in some instances simply held, it places the wearer in, or connects them to, the spirit or wraith realm. We see this in a number of instances throughout *The Lord of the Rings*, with Isildur, Gollum, Gandalf, and Frodo (History of the Ages (b) 2021). As such, it makes them invisible to those not similarly placed. As Gandalf points out to the hobbits, repeated wearing of the ring leads to permanent entrapment there, similar to the Ringwraiths and Barrow-wights (Day 1993). It would appear that Tom, by his nature, possesses all the inherent powers of the ring, including interdimensionality, though there is no metaphysical attachment as is the case with Sauron. He therefore has no use for it, and is able to reject it off-hand. Tom is the ultimate kill-switch to the war of the ring in that he possesses power in relation to it, unlike any other being on Middle-earth apart from Sauron. But there is no clear definition of that power. This is why Tolkien has presented Gandalf's remarks at the Council of Elrond in regards to Tom Bombadil as equivocating rather than emphatic. Gandalf, like the reader, does not know Tom's true nature and is only guessing at the extent of his power. He is an enigma both to those within Middle-earth and the readers without.

· *Spirit nature*: Tom is both spirit and corporeal (possesses a body). Tolkien hints at this in a rather humorous way when Frodo informs us that Tom, after working for a period in heavy rain, returns to the house dry as a bone, with only his boots wet. As noted above, Tom's spirit nature is also exposed when he wears the Ring of Power and does not disappear. Because he is already part of that 'other system', the Ring of Power therefore has no perceivable or actual effect on him. He can make it disappear by transporting it into the spirit realm with him, just as it seemingly disappears when Frodo and others put it on. The only difference is that Tom does not disappear when he wears it. Also, as a spirit, he can see Frodo when the latter wears the ring and appears invisible to those around him, apart from those who are also in the spirit realm, such as Ringwraiths and the Eye of Sauron.

· *Physicality*: When freeing the hobbits from the Barrow, Tom physically destroys part of the ancient structure with his bare hands. He later picks up a hoard of treasure and then removes the Barrow-wight's spell by placing it on top of the mound and offering it without restriction to the hobbits. He spends his time day and night creating and has almost boundless energy, which is suggestive of great physical strength. An element of his Elvish name Iarwain Ben-adar refers to his youthful vitality, or physical strength.

· *Fearlessness*: 'He has no fear', says Goldberry in regards to Tom, and goes on to note rather strangely that nobody has ever caught him. Both once again point to a spiritual nature;he has no fear as he cannot be physically captured or harmed, and he cannot be caught as he is a powerful, immortal spirit, capable of swift movement through space and perhaps time. As such, he bears the physical and mental strength to ward off attack. This is relevant to the hobbits who, when they first encounter Tom, are fearful and being chased by Black Riders. He imbues them with some of his energy as is evident by Frodo's fight against entrapment by the Barrow-wight, and later effort to ward off the Black Riders at the ford. Tom is able to take fear away, and his horse Fatty Lumpkin similarly removes the fear from the ponies used by the hobbits. Bombadil lives in a Middle-earth wracked by fear. The fact that he has no fear points to a higher purpose, for the only other entity in Tolkien's mythology to be without fear would be Eru, the Creator. We are further told that Tom existed prior to Melkor bringing fear into the world.

· *Infiltrate dreams*: Tom and Goldberry are able to enter into dreams and communicate with the sleeper. For example, when Pippin is having a nightmare, the following words come into his head, which reflect earlier statements by Tom and Goldberry: 'Fear nothing! Have peace until the morning! Heed no nightly noises!' On one occasion Bombadil also stimulates the dream of Frodo in regards to the fate of Gandalf on the Tower of Orthanc, recently imprisoned there by Saruman. Of the six dreams within

The Lord of the Rings described in any detail, four take place in the house of Tom Bombadil.

· *Prophetic:* Tom is able to see the future and stimulate prophecy. He knows that four hobbits are coming to his house, and prepares a room accordingly. He instils in the mind of Frodo a dream regarding his ultimate fate and journey to the Undying Lands. Merry also has a prophetic dream relating to water whilst in Bombadil's house. According to his own words, and those of Tolkien, Tom is aware of the past, present and future, in a manner beyond mere intuition.

· *Positive Nature*: Tom is a bastion of positivity within a decidedly bleak and fearful world of death and destruction at the hands of Sauron and his minions, including Ring Wraiths, Orcs and Saruman the White. He shows that evil may be present on Middle-earth, but it can be resisted and conquered. He also reminds the hobbits that there are more important things in Arda than Sauron's ring and the quest to destroy it. He does this when he is able to make the ring disappear and present himself as impervious to its influence. This is a significant reference to the role of spirituality and religious belief in a physical world of suffering, doubt and fear. Bombadil reflects the great spiritual leaders of history, such as Jesus Christ and Buddha, in projecting peace and promoting mindfulness and internal enlightenment, rather than focussing on a temporal quest for power – in taking 'a vow of poverty' as Tolkien puts it. We see this not only in the blatant quest for power by figures such as Sauron and Saruman, but also in misplaced efforts to destroy evil, which can lead to damnation (Perkins 1975). This latter sentiment is reflected in both Gandalf and Galadriel's rejection of the Ring of Power, and Boromir's attempt to take the ring from Frodo. Tom dispenses a positive energy which is invigorating, inspiring and emboldening.

· *Persuasion*: Tom is able to make Frodo speak openly and freely like never before. He unleashes the truth, as in a confessional, and displays empathy in the face of such revelations.

· *Knowledge*: as a timeless, ageless immortal being and resident of Arda, Tom has a long memory and wide circle of friends and informants. For example, in an early draft Tolkien writes that he has a complete knowledge of the history of the hobbits and receives updates from his friends Farmer Maggot and Galdor the Elf. He has, over time, travelled widely and been known throughout Middle-earth, as revealed by the comments of Elrond and Treebeard, and the numerous names he has acquired. Tom's knowledge is unbound.

· *Time Dilation*: During the second day at the house of Tom Bombadil and Goldberry, Frodo noted that time seemed to stand still as the hobbits sat with Tom and he told them stories and offered counsel. Whilst only a single day passed, to Frodo it felt much longer. Whether this was a mere perception, or a reality induced by Bombadil, is unknown, though the latter is likely. A similar thing happened when the hobbits visited the Elf haven of Lothlorien, with Elvish time flowing variously quicker or slower than normal time. It seems that Tom was able to slow down time in order to lengthen the period during which he could provide assistance and counsel to the hobbits. Once again, this is a device Tolkien has introduced and used with purpose.

Tom Bombadil's extensive suite of powers points to a being of decided difference and uniqueness compared to other Middle-earth beings. He is similar, in some ways, to the Lucifer character in the similarly named *Netflix* television series – therein a son of God, with divine powers, though, unlike Tom, vulnerable in the presence of a Goldberry equivalent and grappling with the realities of being human and the selective use of those powers.

So what is he, this Tom Bombadil character? The official Tolkien Estate website tells us that Bombadil 'originated outside the legends of Arda', perhaps in reference to his substantive origin in the 1934 *The Adventures of Tom Bombadil*, though also hinting at a more significant background (Lauzon 2017). Tolkien's 1937 letter to Stanley Unwin identified Bombadil as, at that stage, a representation of 'the spirit of the (vanishing) Oxford and Berkshire countryside' – the first such reference to him as other than Middle-earth flesh and blood, though this is an earth-based reference and limited as such in its application to the world of *The*

Lord of the Rings. This pitch to the publisher can be read as separating Bombadil from what Tolkien had created up to that point in time in relation to an evolving mythology. He was also perhaps seeking to tie him in with Britain's ancient Celtic origins, as a mythical character (Seth 2015). Though Tolkien wrote about the world outside of Middle-earth in letters to his publishers and friends, the world was only revealed in any detail after his death, within *The Silmarillion*, *The History of Middle-earth* series and the *Unfinished Tales* compilation. A few elements were also contained within the Appendices to *The Lord of the Rings*. The designation of Bombadil as an earthly spirit, or spirit of the earth (Arda), is widely disseminated and, on the surface, a reasonable explanation. However, it is based on a twentieth century analogy rather than a Third Age or mythical reality and does not explain his aforementioned suite of powers. The enigma therefore remains, despite the best efforts of researchers, scholars and fans to lift the imposed veil of mystery.

CHAPTER 5:

Creation, Catholicism and the One

om Bombadil is not catalogued, defined or fully incorporated within the suite of characters created by Tolkien and as revealed in *The Lord of the Rings* and *The Silmarillion*. As such, every attempt to fit him in has, to date, failed. Whilst he is commonly assumed by students of Tolkien's legendarium to be a Maia or Vala, another interesting assessment is that provided by an anonymous 2013 blog post which presented a logical, though complex argument for Bombadil as the incarnate (i.e. living) spirit of the so-called Music of the Ainur (*Ranger from the North* 2013). In order to understand what the Music of the Ainur is, and its significance in regards to Tom Bombadil, one needs to go beyond *The Lord of the Rings* into the world of *The Silmarillion*, and more specifically its first chapter, or creation myth equivalent - the *Ainulindalë*. The first line of that work reads:

There was Eru, the One, who in Arda is called Ilúvatar. (Silmarillion)

'The One' is the legendarium equivalent of the monotheistic God of Tolkien's Christian faith. Therein this 'One' God is actually three entities in the form of what Tolkien, and the Catholic Church, refers to as the 'Blessed Trinity' comprising God the Father, the Word of God (Logos) or God the Son, and God the Holy Spirit or Holy Ghost (Joyce 1912, Letters 131). Each element of the Trinity is distinct but not separate. They are one in being, but three in person. The Trinity is the greatest mystery of the Catholic faith, with its true nature having been the subject of debate and philosophical discussion over the millennia. In many ways it is analogous to the position of Tom Bombadil within Tolkien's legendarium, with both being mysterious and enigmatic; endlessly discussed but never fully revealed.

The idea of one God existing in a tripartite form as the Father, Word (Logos) / Son and Holy Spirit / Holy Ghost does not, on the surface, make sense. God the Father is easily acknowledged, with the use of signifiers such as creator, the Father, and the Almighty involving singular concepts which are universally applied in a variety of religions and belief systems. The terms are recognised and therefore resonate, especially as most references to God are in the singular, though Hinduism has no limit to the number of gods that can be venerated, and Greek mythology has a large suite of gods. Buddhism does not use the term. Believers and non-believers readily understand the notion of God as the deemed original creator of all things, even if they do not believe or appreciate the complexity of that statement. It is a metaphysical concept which can easily be presented in those terms. Likewise, the Word of God (Logos) or God the Son is comprehended due to the widely promulgated belief in his historic manifestation as Jesus Christ and the detailed account of his life presented within the New Testament section of the *Bible*, alongside ancient chroniclers such as Romano-Jewish historian Josephus (37 – c.100). This historicity assists in general acceptance, or at least understanding and awareness outside of belief. Though separate, Jesus Christ is, according to the doctrine of the Catholic Church, also God. And once again, the idea of God the Father and God the Son resonates with non-Christians, though as two separate entities. The existence of the Holy Spirit, or Holy Ghost, and its place within the Blessed Trinity, is not so easily explained or understood, though it is readily accepted by followers of the Catholic faith and an important part of the associated ceremony and practice.

For Catholics the concept and history of the Holy Spirit is complex. It has been the subject of much theological discussion over time, since even before the beginning of the church of Christ. As such, it remains so to this day (Wainwright 1962, Carter 1974). The Holy Spirit is described throughout the Old and New Testament sections of the *Bible* as a spirit or ghost-like entity that exists both within and without individuals and beings, and assists them in the fight for goodness against evil. It is often associated with the notion of the *grace* of God. American author Edmund Fuller had noted in 1968 with regards to *The Lord of the Rings*:

A theology contains the narrative rather than being contained by it. Grace is at work abundantly in the story. (Isaacs and Zimbardo 1868)

The Holy Spirit, though obviously a powerful entity, does not dominate or enforce its will. Amongst its many roles, it assists, and provides counsel and direction. There was never any definitive manifestation of the Holy Spirit in the *Bible*, though it was presented therein as variously within a person, an external spirit, a power, or something fluid-like and flowing. According to the *Bible* there was also a close relationship between Jesus Christ and the Holy Spirit during the former's earthly existence. Therein the Holy Spirit was physically seen twice: the first time as a dove floating above the head of Jesus when he was being baptised (Luke 3:21-23), and the second time as a number of distinct flames, or tongues of fire, hovering above the heads of the 120 disciples gathered at the Pentecost feast held 50 days after Jesus is said to have died on the cross at Calvary and ascended into Heaven. The appearance of the Holy Spirit is described therein as follows:

When the day of Pentecost had come, they were all together in one place. And suddenly a sound came from Heaven like the rush of a mighty wind, and it filled all the house where they were sitting. And there appeared to them tongues as of fire, distributed and resting on each one of them. And they were all filled with the Holy Spirit and began to speak in other tongues. (Acts of the Apostles 2:1-13)

The wind, flames of fire, and speaking in different languages, or tongues, are all elements traditionally associated with the Holy Spirit. They are also presented by Tolkien throughout *The Lord of the Rings* in a number of forms. For example, at the Bruinen river ford where Frodo and his companions eventually encounter the Black Riders, these agents of Sauron, who somewhat strangely have an aversion to water, baulk at crossing. However, in an element added after the initial draughting, at the instigation of Elrond the waters rise up and consume them, allowing the hobbits to escape. Tolkien describes the scene as follows:

Dimly Frodo saw the river below him rise, and down along its course there came a plumed cavalry of waves. White flames seemed to Frodo to flicker on their crests and he half fancied that he saw amid the water white riders upon white horses with frothing manes. The three Riders that were still in the midst of the Ford were overwhelmed: they disappeared, buried suddenly in the angry foam. Those that were behind drew back in dismay. With his last failing senses Frodo heard cries, and it seemed to him that he saw, beyond the Riders that hesitated on the shore, a shining figure of white light; and behind it ran small shadowy forms waving flames, that flared red in the grey mist that was falling over the world. (LOTR)

White and red, free-floating flames reflect an important element in both Christian doctrine and Tolkien's mythology, namely, the Secret Fire, or Flame Imperishable which, in *The Silmarillion,* is the active creative force. The flame also persists as a prominent motif within Christian religions as a symbol of the Holy Spirit. According to Catholic doctrine, the Holy Spirit, like Jesus Christ and God the Father, is God, part of the one true God, or 'the One' which in Tolkien's cosmology is present in the form of Eru. However, therein the tripartite nature is not specifically revealed. Within *The Silmarillion* we primarily see the work of the 'God the Father' figure in the form of Eru, and to a lesser degree the Holy Spirit through the Secret Fire or Flame Imperishable. God the Son is absent, as is also the case within the Old Testament section of the *Bible.* Nevertheless, and in addition, Tolkien's use of the term Eru in reference to 'the One' entails the Trinity as a whole. It is also rather confusingly used in conjunction with the term for the God the Father figure as two root words combined to form the commonly used Eru Ilúvatar, or simply Ilúvatar in reference to the singular 'Father of All' on Arda (Tolkien 1980, Kocher 1985, The One Ring 2003, Tolkien Gateway 2017). It can be said that whilst Eru refers to the Blessed Trinity aka God aka the One, the term Eru Ilúvatar, or simply Ilúvatar, refers to the God the Father figure alone, in an earthly / Middle-earth / Arda context.

Tolkien was a devout Roman Catholic, well versed in the church's traditions and doctrines. Following his experiences in World War

I, and his observation of the subsequent disillusionment and move from traditional religions by large sections of Western society disenchanted with their fate in life, he sought to plant an immortal seed by producing an epic, popular mythology (legendarium) which had at its core Catholic doctrine (Jungmyung 2016, Rogers 2018). *The Lord of the Rings* was the result. However, Tolkien himself noted that he was no theologian and therefore his grasp of Christian concepts and their corresponding representations within his work was rudimentary in comparison to contemporary theologians, though learned in hindsight. The incorporation of the Creator within his legendarium was one instance where the author grappled with a blending of the theological and the mythological. Further confusion regarding this issue exists in *The Lord of the Rings* where the term 'the One' is used throughout to refer to Sauron's Ring of Power, as in 'the One Ring' to rule them all. Also, there appears to be no specific reference in the body of the text to 'the One' as in Eru, though Tolkien equivocates in regards to this important issue and elsewhere indicates otherwise. In fact, in a BBC television interview recorded during 1968, he stated that there are 'a couple' of references to 'the One' - as in God and not 'the One' ring - within *The Lord of the Rings*. Unfortunately, he did not specify at that time what they were (Tolkien 1968). One of these references is found in Appendix A's *Tale of Aragorn and Arwen,* whereby the latter, as an immortal Elf, states in regards to death, that it is 'the gift of the One to Man' (LOTR). Immortality is in this instance seen by Arwen as a curse, where one watches loved ones grow old and die. She would much prefer God's gift of life and death i.e., mortality.

The story of the creation of Middle-earth and its subsequent history was important to Tolkien the mythmaker. His view of the interrelated role of God, nature and the fall as presented in the story of Adam and Eve, is seen most especially within *The Silmarillion* and through the Music of the Ainur in the creation of Eä. Therein Eru made use of music and song as a primary form of expression and creation. This equates to the Biblical presentation of the God the Son figure as present at the time of creation in the form of the Word, and later to manifest on Earth in the form of Jesus Christ. The latter does not appear in Tolkien's legendarium as it is set in a pre-Christian time (Kocher 1985).

At one point Tolkien's Eru brought into being the Ainur - holy ones or angels. In turn the Holy Spirit, in the form of the Secret Fire, used its (God's) power of creation to manifest their vision. As Eru stated in *The Silmarillion*:

'And I shall send forth into the void the Flame Imperishable, and it shall be at the heart of the World, and the World shall Be' . . . And suddenly the Ainur saw afar off a light, as it were a cloud with a living heart of flame, and they knew that this was no vision only, but that Ilúvatar had made a new thing: Eä, the World that Is.

And in the *Valaquenta* section of *The Silmarillion* Tolkien writes:

Therefore, Ilúvatar gave to their vision Being, and set it amid the Void, and the Secret Fire was sent to burn at the heart of the World; and it was called Eä. (Silmarillion)

The subsequent process by which the universe was created from the Void was referred to by Tolkien as the Music of the Ainur and is described in the *Ainulindalë*. All of this mirrors the account of creation contained within the Old Testament book of *Genesis*. Therein, everything is created through the word of God, as is "Let there be light" and "Let the earth bring forth vegetation…" (McMurray 2021). This use of words and sound to create, whether it be the word of God within the *Bible*, the pre-Christian Hebrew *Book of Enoch*, or Tolkien's Music of the Ainur, is ultimately reflected in the power of the words and song of Tom Bombadil within *The Lord of the Rings*. Creation through sound is a powerful process which modern science is revealing played a significant role in the creation of the universe (Britt 2005). Tolkien once again mixes fact with fantasy, and myth with religious doctrine to develop an origin story for his legendarium, with *Genesis* and *Enoch* as primary sources (Cook 2017). Once this semi-scientific and doctrinally correct environment has been created, he is then free to proceed with his main aim of story-telling. For this he initially makes use of various angels, which he calls Valar, Maiar and Ainur. Unfortunately, one of the Ainur - Melkor - brought fear into the world and ultimately to Middle-earth through his discordant song (sound). The fight between good - the Ainur - and the evil Melkor (also called Morgoth) and his minions, including Sauron - became a universal and eternal drama, carried on by their children, creations and followers, though with the knowledge of Eru who looked on from afar and did not directly interfere. This is likewise analogous to the action of the God of Tolkien's Catholic faith, who does not directly intervene in the suffering of individuals or take physical form on earth. It gives rise to the eternal question in the face of tragedy – Why does God allow this to happen? This dichotomy of a loving God overseeing a world of suffering lies at the heart of events in *The Lord of the Rings*, just as it did in Tolkien's own life as he experienced the horrors of the Western Front and tragic loss of friends during World War I. Acceptance of suffering also lies at the core of the Buddhist belief system.

The presence of God in the world of Frodo Baggins is thus implicit rather than explicit, and meaningfully so. Within Tolkien's cosmology the Ainur are angels, placed there as equivalents of, for example, the gods of classical Greek mythology; Melkor is the fallen angel Diabolos (Lucifer or the Devil); and there are a number of characters who in their actions reflect the life of Jesus Christ, the earthly embodiment of God the Son. These include Gandalf the Grey who is resurrected as Gandalf the White (prophet), Frodo the ring bearer (priest) and Aragorn (king). The fellowship of the ring is analogous to Christ and his apostles, whilst a number of female figures reference the role of Mary, the mother of Jesus, including Galadriel and Goldberry, the latter most especially with her golden aura. Tolkien utilised such devices to assist those readers who were Catholic and averse to pagan mythology, referring to it as follows:

The cycles begin with a cosmogonical myth: the Music of the Ainur. God and the Valar (or powers: Englished as gods) are revealed. These latter are, as we should say, angelic powers, whose function is to exercise delegated authority in their spheres of rule and government, not creation, making or re-making. They are 'divine', that is, were originally 'outside' and existed 'before' the making of the world. .... On the side of mere narrative device, this is, of course, meant to provide beings of the same order of beauty, power, and majesty as the 'gods' of higher mythology, which can yet be accepted - well, shall we say baldly, by a mind that believes in the Blessed Trinity. (Letter 131)

Thus, Tolkien reveals the Catholic core of *The Lord of the Rings*, created as a work which would rest easy with, and be accepted by, his fellow believers in the Blessed Trinity.

Whilst discussions such as the possible link between Tom Bombadil and the Ainur are informative, the task of identifying him through such a process of elimination is flawed. For example, the reference in both *The Lord of the Rings* and Tolkien correspondence to the 'Dark Lord' has variously been identified as referring to Melkor or the lesser Sauron. If it is to Melkor, as seems likely, then Tom is older than the creation of Middle-earth and the universe with the assistance of the Ainur. This therefore puts him on par with Eru, the Godhead figure of Tolkien's mythology who manifested (created) the Ainur. Yet Tom also appears to be an intimate part of Arda and therefore has been assumed by many to be younger than Melkor and likely a member of the group of beings known as the Valar or the lesser Maiar. This was rejected by correspondent Acarinaro in the *Tom Bombadil's Identity* discussion on the *Fanatics Plaza* website. He noted therein that, regarding the reference to the Dark Lord by Tom Bombadil:

The 'dark under the stars was fearless' only before Melkor came. Therefore, the 'Dark Lord' referred to in Tom's speech cannot be Sauron. It must be Melkor. Therefore, Tom was there before Melkor entered into the world. Given that Melkor is said to be the first of the Ainur to enter, this means that Tom cannot be one of the Ainur. Since all the Valar and all the Maiar are Ainur, this means that Tom cannot be a Maia or Valar. ... It should also be noted that the process of elimination is doomed to fail, as it makes a fundamental assumption that all types of beings in Middle-earth are catalogued. This is untrue. (Fanatics Plaza 2012)

This quote dispenses with all the theories equating Tom Bombadil with the Ainur, Valar and Maiar, and all other known Middle-earth entities. It is also typical of the detailed, often encyclopedic analysis and discussion of Tolkien's legendarium to be found on modern fan-based websites, and outside of traditional academic and literary circles. The enigmatic nature of the Tom Bombadil character has made him one of the most popular topics of consideration on such sites. The *Ainulindalë*, and to a lesser degree the following chapter *Valaquenta*, are important in these discussions as they are nothing less than Tolkien's creation myth, with application to the universe within which the events of *The Hobbit* and *The Lord of the Rings* take place, along with many of the other works published since his death. Comparisons between the book of *Genesis* and *Ainulindalë* are obvious, with the latter reflecting the intimate connection between Tolkien's personal and religious beliefs and his creative output (Kimel 2018). The Oxford professor proved to be a skilful writer and mythmaker, able in most instances to steer away from allegory, unlike his friend C.S. Lewis with the *Narnia* series. Tolkien masks his strongly held religious views beneath timeless tales of fantasy for young and old, in both prose and verse forms. He pointed this out in a piece of correspondence to Father Robert Murray during 1953, just prior to publication of *The Lord of the Rings,* wherein he stated:

The Lord of the Rings is of course a fundamentally religious and Catholic work; unconsciously so at first, but consciously in the revision. That is why I have not put in, or cut out, practically all references to anything like 'religion', to cults or practices, in the imaginary world. For the religious element is absorbed into the story and the symbolism…. As a matter of fact, I have consciously planned very little. (Letter 142)

Here he reveals both the conscious and unconscious processes inherent within his writing, and the fact that he specifically addressed the religious elements both there and in the revision process. This does not mean Tolkien openly highlighted them for the reader, beyond generalised themes such as good versus evil, mortality, the nobility of individual endeavour, and the importance of friendship. In fact, as he informs Father Murray, he meaningfully 'cut out' almost all overt religious references during the editing process so that *The Lord of the Rings* would generally appear secular. A good example is the deletion of Tom's blessing to the hobbits as they part company, which appeared twice in draft form but not in the final version, though Goldberry did use similar words in dispensing a blessing to them. As a result, even those readers raised as Catholics would find it difficult to identify aspects of Tolkien's writing which superficially come across as faith-based, doctrinaire or moralistic preaching. Nevertheless, Catholicism was such an integral part of the man that its teachings could not help but be present, even if placed there unconsciously - the actuality of which the author readily acknowledged in the aforementioned quote. Furthermore, in a 1958 letter to Rhona Beare, Tolkien said of *The Lord of the Rings*:

I have deliberately written a tale which is built on, or out of, certain 'religious' ideas, but is not an allegory of them (or anything else), and does not mention them overtly, still less preach them... (Letter 211)

This proactive masking of religious elements is seen in the treatment of God throughout *The Lord of the Rings*, for as Tolkien noted in a letter to Michael Straight written around January 1956:

There is no embodiment of the One, of God, who indeed remains remote, outside the World, and only directly accessible to the Valar or Rulers. (Letter 181)

This was reiterated in his later letter to Rhona Beare:

The One does not physically inhabit any part of Eä. (Letter 211)

These statements are true when we understand that Tolkien's reference to 'the One' is to the Blessed Trinity. They also lie at the core of arguments against Tom Bombadil's probable God nature. Their truth is not disputed, for Eru Ilúvatar, for example, is not physically present, but exists in the background, in spirit, just as God existed, and exists, in Tolkien's own world. Neither is the pre-Christian Word of God (Logos) manifest, nor the Christian Son of God. A considered reading of Tolkien's statements, however, does not rule out the presence of the Holy Spirit in Middle-earth, either in corporeal or spirit form, such being its very nature. We also see here the tendency by Tolkien to play with words and talk around topics at length, in the academic manner – to bemuse, befuddle and engage in mystifying circumlocution. Such a possibility i.e., the presence in Middle-earth of the Holy Spirit, in singular or multiple forms, is therefore worthy of investigation.

CHAPTER 6:

The Fellowship of the Holy Spirit

It has been argued by one commentator that Tolkien's legendarium is a Christian universe in a pre-Christian (i.e., pre-Jesus Christ) world. This is reasonable considering the seeming absence of a distinct Christ-like figure. In regards to the Holy Spirit, however, that commentator has noted:

...The gifts of the [Holy] Spirit are present, and the Spirit [is] thus abroad, in Tolkien's Middle-earth. This is true despite the fact that no reference is made to the Spirit, and only the one passing reference to God (LOTR III, 342). (Lobdell 2004)

This is what Tolkien hoped for all along, namely, that the book would not be seen as a religious or allegorical work, populated by deities, but would nevertheless reveal religious elements. One such element is the presence of the Holy Spirit on Middle-earth to impart grace upon individuals in their quest to lead a good, 'Christian' life. In meaningfully deleting specific religious references during the final editing stages, whilst at the same time discreetly adding others, he largely achieved this. The previous commentator then goes on to theologically explain away these omissions, or excisions – specifically in reference to the Holy Spirit:

And the lack of such reference is exactly what we should expect. If we understand ... that the Holy Spirit proceeds from the Father and the Son, "neither made nor created but proceeding," then we must see that a theology consistent with this doctrine cannot define the Spirit without knowing the Son. By definition, in a pre-Christian age, Christ the Son cannot be known, and neither therefore can the Holy Spirit. At the same time reference to the Father (in that Person) would be inaccurate .... without reference to the other Persons of the Trinity. (Lobdell 2004)

The fatal flaw to this argument is Tolkien's inclusion of the Holy Spirit in the form of Secret Fire / Flame Imperishable. Lobdell's argument is not convincing, and turns on itself in the final sentence, for apart from containing a number of debatable points, it fails to recognise the Trinity's existence within the Old Testament, pre-Christian era, which records events prior to the earthly manifestation of Jesus Christ. The analysis also points to one of the reasons Tolkien warned against philosophising over the nature of Tom Bombadil, especially if the character represents the writer's unconscious imagination taking him down a path which does not strictly adhere to Christian theology, though remains within the spirit and bounds of the Catholic faith. The fact is, the Holy Spirit does not require the presence of the Son of God in order to appear or influence. On this point Lobdell's argument falls away, both in regard to Catholic belief and Tolkien's legendarium. Lobdell writes about Tom Bombadil, but only in a 'make-shift' manner, for he finds the figure confusing and cites him as Tolkien's 'least successful creation'. His identification of the presence of the Holy Spirit throughout *The Lord of the Rings* is nevertheless of note, though he misses a direct reference to it as the Secret Fire. This occurred in the published report of a personal conversation between Tolkien and Clyde Kilby, wherein the author of *The Lord of the Rings* specifically identified the Secret Fire as the Holy Spirit, thereby revealing one of the many undoubted Catholic elements of his legendarium:

Professor Tolkien talked to me at some length about the use of the word 'holy' in The Silmarillion. Very specifically he told me that the 'Secret Fire sent to burn at the heart of the World' in the beginning was the Holy Spirit. (Kilby 1976)

Tolkien also stated in his Quenya lexicon that Sä, or fire, is a mystic name identified with the Holy Ghost, also known as the Holy Spirit (Tolkien 1915).

The place of 'the One' in Tolkien's legendarium, and most especially within *The Lord of the Rings*, mirrors the Christian reality in that the Blessed Trinity does not exist on earth in a physical or embodied form, but only in belief and through evidence of its work, apart from the brief period on earth of Jesus Christ. It should be noted that one of Tolkien's aforementioned comments in this regard specifically refers to the lack of a physical presence of God on Middle-earth, but does not rule out a spiritual or metaphysical form. And though not directly embodied, it could be argued that 'the One' is indirectly, or symbolically, accessible through a spirit entity such as Tom Bombadil. If Lobdell is arguing that the Holy Spirit is evident throughout the book, then so too, in essence, is 'the One', or the Blessed Trinity.

Another commentator has suggested that Bombadil can be interpreted on a number of levels, as 1) a Dutch doll, 2) a spirit of the earth, 3) as Tolkien himself, and 4) as Adam / Jesus Christ (Beal 2018). There is some veracity to the connection with the fatherless Adam of the biblical book of *Genesis*, however Tom does not suffer a similar, sinful fate and the connection is tenuous. As also is that with the Christ figure, which is largely based on the suggestion that Tom resurrected three of the hobbits from the dead whilst they were entrapped in the barrow. This may or may not be true, though their cold, still bodies suggested as much.

Knowing that *The Lord of the Rings* is a Catholic work, that Tolkien generally masked, but did not remove, and on occasion enhanced this aspect of the narrative, and having looked at the seemingly enigmatic and mysterious nature of Tom Bombadil and of the Holy Spirit, it is therefore understandable that a person steeped in both a knowledge of Tolkien's legendarium and Catholic religious doctrine should see connecting elements which are otherwise hidden to a general, non-Catholic, or even lapsed-Catholic reader. And so it was that in 2012 author Jim Denney suggested without any equivocation that Tom Bombadil is Tolkien's version of the Holy Spirit – an embodiment of God's power, or spirit, in Middle-earth (Denney 2012). According to Denney, he was that part of God – the One – who created the universe through the Music of the Ainur or process of the Secret Fire. Denney was not the first, however, to suggest a link, having been preceded in 2004 by a posting on the *Fanatics Plaza* forum. Therein the anonymous Gilestel posited a connection between Bombadil and the Flame Imperishable, based on Tolkien's comments in *The Lord of the Rings* and an analysis of *The Silmarillion* (Fanatics Plaza 2004). Gilestel noted that Tom predated Melkor and the Ainur, and discussed the sending of the Flame Imperishable to Eä. A subsequent discussion on the forum, which carried over into 2005, largely rejected the idea (Fanatics Plaza 2005). At no point did the correspondents therein make the related connection between the Secret Fire / Flame Imperishable and the Holy Spirit, nor seem cognisant of the Catholic core of *The Lord of the Rings*. Likewise, the 2021 Nerd of the Rings presentation of five Tom Bombadil origin theories begins with a rejection of his connection with the supreme Eru Ilúvatar, reflecting a lack of understanding of Tolkien's Catholicism (Nerd of the Rings 2021). Apart from these instances, as far back as 1979

125

a link was made between Tom Bombadil and the music of the Ainur (aka the Holy Spirit) within a book comprising a Jungian analysis of Tolkien's legendarium. Of Tom Bombadil it was said, therein:

Old Tom is, I venture to speculate, the "hidden melody," the secret tune of The One from which His children took form and grew - the divine tonal DNA! (O'Neil 1979)

In light of these assertions, Tom Bombadil therefore appears to be a manifestation of the Holy Spirit in that he too is ageless, fatherless, powerful in his ability to provide guidance and support, and a pacifist in not enforcing his will upon others, apart from those such as Old Man Willow and the Black Riders who aim to cause harm to sentient beings under his protection. Gandalf criticises Tom for lack of active involvement in the war of the ring, but we can see how it is not his role, or nature, as an embodiment of the Holy Spirit to act in this manner. He is not a warrior, but more a defender and a force to strengthen and embolden the will to defend within sentient beings. He is a provider of grace. Just as the trees of the Old Forest forcefully defend their ground against intruders, so too we see the four hobbits similarly inspired in their journey to destroy the Ring of Power after leaving Tom and Goldberry.

If we support Denney's proposition that Tom Bombadil is a manifestation of the Holy Spirit in Middle-earth at the time of *The*

Lord of the Rings, then we can make a connection between Bombadil as a manifestation of the Secret Fire, and through that the initial and ongoing acts of creation of, and on, Middle-earth. Tom as an earth spirit, or *the* earth spirit, is a subsidiary of this. He informs us that he was in Arda before the various elements were formed, including the sun, moon, oceans, rivers, trees and peoples. As he pursues his work of 'making' in the Old Forest, this represents a continuation of that process of creation. The proposition also ties in with a number of fan sites that raise the idea of Bombadil as closely related to Eru. One of the most considered is an anonymous posting from the *Science Fiction & Fantasy Forum* during February 2021, addressing the question as to what Gandalf intended to chat about with Tom Bombadil when he went to meet him in October 3019, after departing from the hobbits:

There's also the theory to consider, that Tom Bombadil was some kind of aspect of Iluvatar; a way to have a perspective in the world without interfering himself. This means it could be just a report on the situation to his superior. The power of Tom Bombadil had no match. The ring was a thing so complex, so powerful, that [there] were none in the world able to undo it, or even completely control it (except for Sauron in this regard). None but Tom. Tom could not be corrupted by the ring, could not be controlled or tempted. Even more impressively, he could change the ring, control it, play with it in a technically impossible way. So, I always imagined this talk between him and Gandalf as a discussion about "Is the work really

done now? What is left to do? What are the possibilities for the future; is it really rid of Melkor and Sauron's influence for good?".
Should I stay or should I go now?

This is the most logical reason encountered to date for the meeting. However, most commentators reject the idea of Tom being Eru / God on the basis of Tolkien's draft comments in response to the Peter Hastings letter. The latter has been misread as emphatically refuting the suggestion that Tom was God, or in any way connected with 'the One', when in fact this was not the case.

Bombadil as the Holy Spirit, or a lesser manifestation of the Holy Spirit, addresses a number of significant issues created by Tolkien around the character, some of which have been referred to above. It also helps explain the aforementioned extensive suite of powers allocated to Bombadil by Tolkien. However, in order to consider it more fully, one needs to understand the religious context and important role specific elements of Catholicism played in Tolkien's life, alongside the nature of the Holy Spirit itself as he would have experienced it. We can start with three basic acclamations of Roman Catholic faith that Tolkien would have professed on a regular, perhaps daily, basis as he said prayers or attended religious rituals. The first - the so-called *Sign of the Cross* - reads:

In the name of the Father, and of the Son and of the Holy Spirit, Amen. (Matthew 28:19)

With these words, and the corresponding signing of the cross with a single motion of the hand, Catholics begin and end prayer and ceremony, including the central liturgical ritual known as the mass. Also stated at the beginning of the mass, and after the sign of the cross, is the following antiphon:

The grace of our Lord Jesus Christ and the love of God and the fellowship of the Holy Spirit be with you all. (2 Corinthians 13:14)

The use and expression of the term 'fellowship' in the Catholic faith is evident in the unity and diversity of Tolkien's Blessed Trinity. Outside of the church it more generally refers to companionship, friendship and the camaraderie associated with a journey. There may be a link between the Catholic use of the term, the gifts imbued by the Holy Spirit, and Tolkien's own Fellowship of the Ring, though nowhere does the author specifically identify any such link. The language of Elrond as he bids the Fellowship of the Ring on its way is very reminiscent of elements of the Catholic liturgy.

In regards to the sign of the cross, it can be seen in the Peter Jackson film version of *The Lord of the Rings* as Aragorn sits over the body of the recently deceased Boromir and says a prayer. This simple sentence and action is one of the basic statements of Catholic faith and a core element of the rite of baptism which introduces a person into the Catholic church. It is more fully developed and proclaimed within the *Nicene Creed*, which is a centrepiece of the mass. The latter reads, in part:

I believe in one God, the Father almighty, creator of Heaven and earth, of all things seen and unseen. I believe in one Lord, Jesus Christ, the only Son of God, born of the Father before time began, God from God, Light from Light, true God from true God, begotten but not made, one in being with the Father. Through him all things were made. For us men and for our salvation he came down from Heaven, and by the power of the Holy Spirit was born of the Virgin Mary, and became man.... I believe in the Holy Spirit, the Lord, the giver of life, who proceeds from the Father and the Son, and who, with the Father and the Son, is worshipped and glorified. He has spoken through the prophets... (Catholic Online 2017).

For students of Tolkien, who was a great fan of the Latin rendition of the mass, the text of the *Nicene Creed* bears similarities in tone, content and rhythm with the secular language of the *Ainulindalë* and the early chapters of *The Silmarillion*. The Blessed Trinity, as outlined in the three texts above – the Sign of the Cross, the antiphon and the *Nicene Creed* - can be seen to reside at the very heart of Christian belief and teaching. In order to better understand *The Lord of the Rings* it therefore helps, though is not necessary, to understand and be aware of this concept of the Blessed Trinity and its meaning to the author.

As a devout Catholic, Tolkien believed in, and promulgated throughout his life, the doctrine of the church. It is well known, for example, that he played a role in the conversion of fellow writer C.S. Lewis to Catholicism. However, he also went to pains to point out that whilst his religious beliefs were core to his identity, he was a writer and creator of myth for a general audience. His creative output was not meant to be overtly religious, let alone Catholic, allegorical or preachy. As a consequence, we have seen how the process of writing *The Lord of the Rings* involved two basic elements: (1) the drafting, which could be a combination of both conscious and unconscious imaginative thought; and (2) a rewriting or revision, in which ideas would be expanded upon, internal consistency developed, and overt religious elements excised or, where added, were masked, whilst general Catholic themes and elements were embedded throughout the work and symbolism refined. As noted above, Tolkien referred to this process within his correspondence, though even there he did not always open up or fully explain what he had written, even if he knew himself.

In creating a new mythology for his homeland, Tolkien was mindful of achieving a secular outcome through presentation of universal truths in the storytelling (Lobdell 1981). The ultimate and continuing success of *The Hobbit* and *The Lord of the Rings* is testament to this. It could be said that the vast majority of Tolkien scholarship and discussion does not come from, or evidence an awareness of, a Christian or Catholic perspective. But having achieved this stripping of overt religious sentiment, Tolkien did not abandon his Catholic faith. Far from it. It may have been hidden within his creative output but, as he again tells us, he left clues for those with a mind to look, and thereby achieve a deeper understanding of the work.

The current author, though raised a Catholic, only came to consider the religious aspects of Tolkien's fictional account of Middle-earth when all attempts to understand the Tom Bombadil character failed to provide consistent and comprehensive answers. However, in developing an awareness of the heretofore hidden Catholic perspective, revelations were plenty. For example, Frodo's bearing of the ring to Mount Doom could be equated to Jesus Christ's carrying of the cross of crucifixion on Calvary. The reference to Tom Bombadil being 'fatherless' also gains meaning within a religious context. For example, the Elves know him as Iarwain Ben-adar, which means 'oldest and fatherless,' and according to Elrond he is 'older than old.' As the *Nicene Creed* points out, the Holy Spirit was not - unlike Jesus Christ - born of the Father, and therefore is in one sense, along with God the Father, ultimately the only entity in the Catholic universe who can be deemed fatherless. This may explain the significance of Tolkien's repeated reference to Tom as fatherless, both in correspondence and within *The Lord of the Rings*. It is a primary pointer to revealing the true nature of Tom Bombadil. The suggestion that Tom is a corporeal incarnation of Eru is brought to mind when Goldberry states with regards to her husband that 'He is'. We are initially drawn to a comparison with God's statement to Moses in the *Bible* that 'I am', or 'I am that I am.' Yet Tolkien seemingly rejects this assertion with the comment that:

If you say 'he is' there must be more than one, and created (sub) existence is implied. (Letter 153)

Tolkien, a professor of philology, frequently uses language to baffle his readers and correspondents. Here he does not lie, and neither does he simplify or aid in comprehension with regards to the Catholic subtext of his work. Instead, he answers the question in a manner which does not address the God issue, but rather deals with it as a non-Godly, sentient being who is one of many. However, a close reading of the extract and the full draft of Hastings' letter, reveals that Tolkien is cryptically making a connection between Bombadil and the Creator within the context of the Blessed Trinity. God's statement to Moses can be read in this context, with 'I am' implying a unique and primary reference to the tripartite One. To paraphrase Tolkien: If you say 'He is' there must be more than one – as there is with the Blessed Trinity in the form of the Father, Son and Holy Ghost – and it, or they, are no longer primary but were created, as is the case with all beings apart from God. By Goldberry stating in regards to Tom that 'He is', Tolkien also points out that this usually also implies a sub-creation, yet we are told, rather forcefully, that he is fatherless and therefore neither creation or sub-creation – he just 'is'. These statements can also be reconciled if we assume that Goldberry's statement 'He is' is simply the first part of the immediately following statement 'He is the Master' and therefore not of specific relevance to Tom Bombadil's godly nature, as has been interpreted to date.

Most commentators fail to recognise this tripartite nature of God. It is true that Tom Bombadil is not a manifestation or embodiment of Ilúvatar, or the God the Father figure, and neither is he of God the Son who nowhere appears in Tolkien's legendarium. But when we analyse Tom's presence in *The Lord of the Rings,* we see that Tolkien has allocated to him many characteristics which equate to 'the One'. Therefore, the only thing he can be, as part of the Blessed Trinity, is the Holy Spirit, which in Tolkien's legendarium takes the form of the Secret Fire / Flame Imperishable and which, in turn, is responsible for all things created. Various elements point to this:

· Tom is a creator whose primary source of communication is song. He creates and makes changes to the world around him with it and through it. This reflects the power of Eru (God / The Blessed Trinity) in manifesting the vision of the Ainur to complete the process of creation through the Music of the Ainur. Only Eru has the power of 'creation, making and re-making', through the original creative force of the Flame Imperishable / Secret Fire or the Holy Spirit. Therefore Tom, as a creator, is a manifestation of

134

the Holy Spirit and the so-called Music of the Ainur. He is a master of creation and of the earth (Arda) but not over individual free will. As such, he is not 'master of the Riders that come from the Black Land' as they answer to, and are under the influence of, Sauron. He is only 'master of water, wood and hill', i.e. of creation. The 9th century Latin hymn *Veni Creator Spiritus* (*Come, Holy Spirit, Creator Come*) emphasises this aspect of the Holy Spirit and may have been one of Tolkien's influences in regards to both the content and structure of the original 1934 *The Adventures of Tom Bombadil* verse. He was aware of the hymn and referred to it in his 1962 edition of the translation of the medieval *Ancrene Wisse* (Tolkien 1962b, Saward Morrill and Tomko 2013).

· Tom is deemed 'Eldest' and 'fatherless' by Tolkien, whilst Ilúvatar is deemed 'Father of All'. Yet Bombadil is twice referred to by Tolkien as 'fatherless'. Therefore, both Tom Bombadil and Ilúvatar are on an equal footing, with no beginning and no end. As the Holy Spirit was not born of God the Father or God the Son, but is equal with them and proceeds from them, he is fatherless. The Trinity, by its nature, is also Eldest in the fact of existing at the beginning of time. Therefore, Tom (i.e., the Holy Spirit) and Ilúvatar are the same in that they are aspects of Eru – 'the One' - God.

· In two early drafts of *The Lord of the Rings*, Tom imparts a blessing upon the hobbits when they part company. This points to Tolkien's initial consideration of his godly, Christian nature.

· Tom has the power to communicate with living entities and assist them. He possesses a spiritual dimension which is beyond the realm of life in Middle-earth. The *Bible* states: '*But you shall receive power when the Holy Spirit comes upon you*' (Acts of the Apostles 1:8). Tom is a powerful entity who, in a subtle manner, is able to empower those who seek his assistance and bear the right intentions. He empowers the party of hobbits en route to Mordor and Mount Doom.

· Tom can call up the wind, which is a traditional sign of the Holy Spirit. He is also able to abate it, as he does when the hobbits are trapped by the Willowman. This aspect of the book is discussed at length in the article *A Wind from the West: The Role of the Holy Spirit in Tolkien's Middle-earth* (Hartley 2012).

· Tom is not affected by Middle-earthly forces such as the Ring of Power. He is 'Outside' of this influence and, as Tolkien has noted, the use of that term refers to the Divine, Eru or the Blessed Trinity.

· Tom displays elements of a dimensionless spirit. He can seemingly travel through space in an instant, and he can project – and receive – thoughts in a similar manner. For example, he communicates directly with the hobbits through song when they are together, and when he leaves them and his voice is out of reach, he projects to a degree whereby the song remains audible and clear, despite the physical separation. Tom is also impervious to the effects of the Ring of Power in forcing him into the spirit realm, as he is already a spirit (Reilly 1968, Scheps 1975). Tom appears real, but Tolkien has made him the manifestation of a spirit.

· Tom's distinctive red face is reminiscent of Saint Stephen the martyr whose face was bright and said to be filled with the Holy Spirit (Acts of the Apostles 6:8 – 8:3).

· Tom projects an energy which is positive and renews the spirit and body of others. This is one of the traditional roles of the Holy Spirit.

· Tolkien saw the Holy Spirit as integral to goodness and hope on Arda. Tom Bombadil, like the Holy Spirit, exists to help one escape evil and find and embrace goodness. Just as the Holy Spirit instils grace in beings such as the author, so also Tom instils grace in the hobbits.

· It could be suggested that Goldberry is Tolkien's manifestation of that fluid-like element of the Holy Spirit noted in the *Bible*. Her intimate connection with Tom, and similar suite of powers, suggests a unity between the two. That unity may go beyond the traditional husband and wife role initially presented in the 1934 verse.

· Tom provides the hobbits with the seven gifts that are traditionally associated with the Holy Spirit, as opposed to the generally more well-known 7 Deadly Sins. These gifts include:

Wisdom – as a being who is immortal and with a wide circle of contacts, Tom is knowledgeable, wise and referred to as a master by Goldberry and Frodo. He provides the hobbit party with sage advice. His wisdom is likely one of the reasons Gandalf seeks him out following the destruction of the Ring of Power.

Understanding – Tom takes time, and literally makes time, to sit down with the hobbits and listen to their story. He shows understanding of their plight, and an empathy which is acknowledged by them. Despite the brevity of their encounter, Tom leaves a lasting impression upon the hobbits.

Counsel – Tom speaks of providing counsel to the hobbits as soon as he identifies their need for such. He allocates time to this, spending a whole day in counsel with them.

Fortitude (courage) – Tom's example in overcoming Old Man Willow and the Barrow-wights emboldens the hobbits to continue on their journey and face foes such as Ringwraiths and Orcs. They all subsequently display courage in the quest to destroy the Ring of Power, ably assisted by the weapons Tom provided to them.

Knowledge – Tom displays a great deal of knowledge about the world around him, and uses his time with the hobbits to pass some of that knowledge on in order to assist them in achieving their goal. He does this through direct speech, song, stories and lucid dreams.

Piety (reverence) – Tom does not utter a harsh word towards anyone, and is gracious in his dealings with the hobbits. His piety is not obvious in his words but rather in his actions and very being. Reference to him as 'the Master' also reflects this high standing he is able to engender.

Wonder - As Donaghy notes, '[Bombadil] is the contemplative hermit of Middle-earth, knowing the names of the living things and the "tune" for each of them. A quote from Pope John Paul II comes to mind: "Faced with the sacredness of life and of the human person, and before the marvels of the universe, wonder is the only appropriate attitude" (Donaghy 2006). The same author notes that Tom provides grace to the hobbits, in the form of assistance and kindness.

Tom Bombadil can therefore be said to represent the manifestation on Arda of the Flame Imperishable / Secret Fire / Holy Spirit. Tolkien had made reference to the Holy Spirit in the Quenya lexicon as far back as 1915, wherein individual names and root forms for members of the Blessed Trinity were devised (Tolkien 1915). They included:

- *Atar* for Father, which eventually gave rise to Ilúvatar;

- *Io Yon* or *Eruion* for God the Son;

- *Fairë aista*, *Aina Fairë*, or *Airëfëa* for the Holy Spirit, with *fëa* the word for soul or spirit;

- *Aina Neldië* for the Holy Trinity itself.

As Tolkien noted, his legendarium, and with it *The Silmarillion* and *The Lord of the Rings*, proceeded primarily from his construction of mythical languages. They formed the very foundation of the aforementioned fictional works. The complexity and sheer breadth of this undertaking was one of the reasons for the lengthy gestation period of *The Lord of the Rings* and problems in securing publication of *The Silmarillion*. Tolkien was immensely frustrated that the project he had been working on since the beginning of World War I would not be published in the chronological order he desired. Therefore, the significance of the root language and words was diminished and a true understanding of all that was contained within *The Lord of the Rings* was not possible. Therein the importance of Tom Bombadil was one of the casualties, as was its connection to Tolkien's creation myth and aspects of The One.

Within *The Lord of the Rings* there is a single, specific reference to the Secret Fire or Holy Spirit, and it involves Gandalf. As he faces the Balrog of Khazad-dûm he utters the words: 'I am a servant of the Secret Fire.' This is just prior to the fall into the abyss on 15 January 3019, which culminates in his subsequent death ten days later on 25 January following pursuit of the Balrog, and resurrection on 14 February. Prior to this, Gandalf had mentioned his use of 'light and flame' in fighting the Ringwraiths at Weather Top on 3 October 3018, just before meeting up with the hobbits. After facing the Balrog and dying, Gandalf the White is now part of the spirit realm, like Bombadil. The connection can therefore be drawn between Gandalf, 'servant of the Secret Fire', and Tom Bombadil as the embodiment of the Secret Fire, or Holy Spirit, on Arda. There are of course deeper theological connotations to this connection. However, it is a generalised context and reveals the method by which Tolkien subtly imbued his mythology with Christian philosophy. For example, in the initial drafting stages Gandalf merely falls into a ditch and stream as he battles the Balrog, and there is no death. In the redrafting, and as Tolkien pointed out, subtle religious elements were added, such that Gandalf is killed and, later, resurrected, or born again, like Jesus Christ, the Son of God. This episode with the Balrog also provides answers to some of the mystery surrounding Tom Bombadil – answers which are not discoverable outside of the context of Catholic doctrine. Furthermore, during the visit of the hobbits to Tom's house, his wife Goldberry, in answer to a question from Frodo about who he is, states: 'Tom Bombadil is the Master,' and 'He is the Master of wood, water and hill.' When the party of hobbits sits down to dinner, Tolkien refers to 'Goldberry and the Master' seated at either end of the table. After listening to Tom speaking, Frodo opens a question to him with the words: 'Did you hear me calling, master?' and later he says, 'Tell us, Master …. about the Willow-man.'

The word 'master' has a specific meaning, one which the author conjures in the mind of the reader through its repeated use within the chapter 'In the House of Tom Bombadil'. It is also a word commonly used by hobbits, and within *The Lord of the Rings* Tolkien uses both lowercase and capitalised 'M' to differentiate significance. In this general context, the relationship of master and servant, or master and pupil, comes to mind. However, based on what is provided within the text, we are not able to go much further. Why does Frodo refer to Tom as master / Master, and what does Goldberry imply when she simply calls him 'the Master'? This reference is not adequately explained by Tolkien within *The Lord of the Rings* and is not therefore easily understood. However, it was obviously put there for a reason and, like other elements of the book - and to use Tolkien's own words - it is likely one of many such mysteries 'not without pointers to a solution' (Letter 190). Therefore, if we look elsewhere within *The Lord of the Rings* and beyond for such pointers, as the author suggests, we may come to glean his intent with regards to the use of the word. The master : servant relationship could apply, for example, to Tom Bombadil and Gandalf, with the latter identifying himself as 'a servant of the Secret Fire', aka a servant of the Holy Spirit, aka a servant of Tom Bombadil, who can therefore be seen as 'the Master'. It may also explain why, at the end of *The Lord of the Rings*, Gandalf leaves the hobbits to meet with Tom. This has long caused readers to wonder what Gandalf wanted to say to him, hear from him, or otherwise gain from such a meeting, especially in light of

Gandalf's discouraging statements in respect of Tom at the Council of Elrond. The answer may reside in the existence of Bombadil as an allegorical manifestation of the Holy Spirit. Bombadil is revealed in this form not through a process of elimination, but rather by inclusion and direct reference to what Tolkien has written and said, both in regard to a Middle-earth context, but also 'Outside' – as in divine - and beyond that as revealed through *The Silmarillion* and the author's own words within his letters and documented conversations.

We have seen that one of the roles of the Holy Spirit is to provide an individual with the power to resist and overcome evil, in the form of grace. It does not, and cannot, of its own volition do that. This explains Tolkien's claim that, in regards to Tom as representative of the goodness inherent in the 'natural pacifist's view':

... there are in fact things with which it cannot cope; and upon which its existence nonetheless depends. Ultimately only the victory of the West will allow Bombadil to continue, or even to survive. Nothing would be left for him in the world of Sauron. (Letter 144)

Therefore, it could be argued that Tom Bombadil, as a manifestation of the Holy Spirit, could not destroy the evil of the Ring of Power, nor have power over Sauron's Black Riders, though he could - and did - assist those fighting against the evil minions of Melkor. If Tolkien had this connection between Tom Bombadil and the Holy Spirit in mind during the development of the character, then it would help explain the variety of powers given to, and displayed by him within *The Lord of the Rings* and other material which references Bombadil. These are in addition to the original substantive manifestation within the 1934 verse *The Adventures of Tom Bombadil*. Though Tolkien had stated – correctly – that there was no physical presence or embodiment of 'the One' in *The Lord of the Rings*, this does not preclude the possibility of Tom Bombadil being 'a particular embodying' of the Holy Spirit for, as Tolkien also said, he represents something that is important and not otherwise represented.

In summary, the case can be made that Tolkien presented to the reader within *The Adventures of Tom Bombadil, The Lord of the Rings* and indirectly through *The Silmarillion*, Tom Bombadil as a manifestation of the Holy Spirit on Arda. This accommodates in whole, or part, the theories which identify him as Eru, Valar, Maiar and the Music of the Ainur. With Tolkien also having stated that the Secret Fire / Flame Imperishable is the Holy Spirit, Tom can be seen as representative of the Secret Fire of creation therein. In turn, Gandalf, as a servant of the Secret Fire, is servant to Tom Bombadil as the Master. Tolkien's narrative would suggest that the wizard was unaware of this prior to his encounter with the Balrog and resurrection as Gandalf the White, and that even in Middle-earth at the end of the Third Age, Tom Bombadil presented as an enigma to those around him.

In placing the encounter between the hobbits and Tom Bombadil at the beginning of *The Lord of the Rings*, Tolkien has created a problem whereby a character that is 'ancient and immortal, and hugely powerful, but essentially indifferent to the travails of the world' breaks, for a time, the reader's 'willing suspension of disbelief' in the larger Middle-earth story (Lockett 2014). The point of Bombadil's intervention in emboldening and preparing the hobbits for their quest is ultimately missed, and the reader returns to the 'Secondary World' as the hobbits bid farewell and head to their encounter with Aragorn (Strider) at Bree. It is only through a Catholic lens that the true purpose of Tom Bombadil, and his partner Goldberry, is revealed, with Tom taking on the mantle of nothing other than the Holy Spirit of the Blessed Trinity i.e., a manifestation of 'the One', or God, in Middle-earth.

CHAPTER 7:

Divinisation and the Divine Story

"He is a strange creature." (Elrond, The Council of Elrond)

Imagine if the greatest possible story you could conceive was true? When I found out in 2019 that Joost van de Loo, a film-maker, was trying to "Find Tom Bombadil", an empirical journey to develop a convincing legal case with all the insurmountable evidence that the Master of Joy was real and truly there, I rang him up immediately and said "I believe too!" Whilst we have not agreed yet if we have indeed found a way of understanding each other linguistically and paradigmatically, it has been a tremendous joy to find someone so passionate about "finding Tom."

So, who is Tom Bombadil to me? To answer this question, I take the theme "Divinisation and the Divine Story" as a way of expressing an artistic intuition, or arc, that could give a meaningful contour to this question. Whilst Joost might claim that I am regressing into a certain mysticism, one that is not of the same technical empiricism of being able to validate the existence of Tom Bombadil (as someone getting "into the plane they just built for you, alongside you and flying with you!" as Joost puts it) I would counter-argue that there are different paths to the same finality. This has been upheld by the Apophatic tradition i.e., the way of Negation – finding God by saying "what He is not", and the Cataphatic tradition i.e., the way of Affirmation – finding God by saying "what He is through affirmation". Whilst J.R.R. Tolkien was not a fan of allegory (in the sense of Lewis' artistic technique) and only stated enigmatically that Tom Bombadil was not the Incarnate God-head of his sub-creation, Joost has argued in his film that perhaps Tolkien "sensed his presence" in the empirically verifiable world. Tolkien experimented with this idea in the *Athrabeth Finrod ah Andreth*, the fourth part of *Morgoth's Ring*, which concerns a future incarnation of Eru (God) into his sub-creation (Tolkien 1993). However, that would be something still to come in his mythos, as it had not as yet happened. The Ring of Power had no influence over Tom, and during the Council of Elrond there was a discussion as to whether the ring should be given to Tom Bombadil. However, the Council decided against following that path.

So, who is Tom? And how can, or could, he be "sensed"? Can Tolkien's sub-creation, or his world-building and creation myths, participate in the empirically verifiable world, and how? To

148

answer this question, and as to if humans can meet Tom Bombadil, I want to pick up on what Joost van de Loo said in an interview about his film. When asked what he would do if he was to hypothetically meet Tom, and what would happen later, he essentially says:

People will come to me and say "Find this character, because this is a fantastic character, or I've written it myself, or I've read about this character or saw him in a film and I really want this character to be found". (van de Loo 2019b)

So, at this juncture of finding the mysterious person at the yearning of all imagination, and willing them to be incarnate before me and touchable, I want to visit the notion of sacramental imagination and the greatest conceivable story. Catholic imagination refers to the Catholic viewpoint that God is present in the whole of creation and in human beings, as seen in its sacramental system whereby material things and human beings are channels and sources of God's grace. The following two theological passages help in understanding this:

1. Plantinga reviving the bishop Anselm's argument about the "greatest conceivable being":

A being's excellence in a particular world depends only on its properties in that world; a being's greatness depends on its properties in all worlds. Therefore, the greatest possible being must have maximal excellence in every possible world. (Internet Encyclopedia of Philosophy 2022)

2. Another Christian apologist, William Lane Craig, characterises Plantinga's argument in a slightly different way:

It is possible that a maximally great being exists. If it is possible that a maximally great being exists, then a maximally great being exists in some possible world. If a maximally great being exists in some possible world, then it exists in every possible world. If a maximally great being exists in every possible world, then it exists in the actual world. If a maximally great being exists in the actual world, then a maximally great being exists. Therefore, a maximally great being exists. (Craig 2022)

These arguments give a good example of the yearning of the human mind for infinity. Karl Rahner, the Jesuit theologian, expressed this yearning in his metaphysical anthropology as what he calls the "supernatural existential":

...the supernatural existential for Rahner is bestowed upon a human being at the initial moment of the human person's existence, in other words at the moment of his or her creation. This follows from the fact that God never had any other intention for human beings than their destination to divine friendship. Hence Rahner states with emphasis that the human person must have this destination "always." It is not as though pure nature existed first in its own right and was then determined. Rather, creation and

determination take place together, though creation belongs to the level of nature, and determination in some way to the level of grace. Nor is the existential simply added to nature; it transforms nature in its coming into being. And the transformation will remain forever, unaltered by anything the person may or may not do subsequently. (Coffey 2004)

This is a remarkable expression of Thomas Aquinas' summation that the human person is destined for eternity, by borrowing the language of experience. He shows that we can "sense" through our mind, imagination, reason and will this capacity for infinity, this capacity for the eternal, and this capacity for a transcendent love.

How does this all link to Tom Bombadil? What if Tom was an imaginative expression of this perfection of nature, made possible by the Incarnation? What if he shows in a person what our nature senses as being its infinite goal?

Tom Bombadil is filled with joy and rapture. He understands the inner songs of nature and his marriage to Goldberry is born of a glorious peace with things being "just as they should be." It seems that in Tom the story is in its fulfilment state. He is not affected by the Ring of Power. This is not opposed to his nature as 'Master' of creation, but rather, is a "perfection from within" of it, that leads to a profound harmony. This kind of profound ecstasy and fulfilment of inner yearning has been consistently taught in the Catholic tradition from writers such as Origen who said in Heaven we would be like spheres or globes, as we will be maximally fulfilled. This is an idea both ancient and new, as in Rahner. The globe is the fulfilment of the supernatural existential, where nature has reached out and grasped infinity within its own unique nature.

Father Michael Gaitley in his book *The One Thing is Three*, does a lot of work in a few lines to explain the destiny of the human person as this yearning for communion with infinity as a story develops (Gaitley 2012). The infinity and the supernatural existential have been made possible by the Incarnation and the Hypostatic Union. The Incarnation is the central belief of Christianity. It is the belief that God became a human being in the historical Person of Jesus Christ. In the Gospels this is expressed as "the Word became flesh" in the Gospel of John. The purpose of God becoming a human being was that all human beings were to become like God and participate in the Divine Life in eternity through the process of becoming holy, also known as divinisation.

The Incarnation and the Hypostatic Union are the two natures in the one Person of Christ; both the human and Divine natures. Human nature is made for elevation into the Divine Nature. I will pick out some of the best lines from Father Michael, on what is known in the Catholic tradition as "Divinisation" i.e., becoming one with God as members of the body of Christ:

Heaven is the participation in the very life of God, as C.S. Lewis says: We will be in the "Great Dance" and with one another. The

point is, we will literally be part of the action ... because we want
something that can hardly be put into words – to be united with the
beauty we see, to pass into it, to receive it into ourselves, to bathe
in it, to become part of it. (Gaitley 2012)

In the most solemn time of the liturgical calendar as Lent reaches Easter, we have had this yearning in our hearts, minds and imaginations for a long time, and probably directly in our experience. We feel like things aren't just quite where they should be yet. We might feel like the "story" just hasn't started yet in our lives or hasn't become fulfilled, in a way that would really make us feel satisfied. It is so hard to be in a place where things just are not where we want them to be yet. We want our deepest desires and yearnings to be fulfilled right now in the flesh. We want to be listened to and understood, and for what we really want, to "become real" in a way that is empirically and spiritually nourishing. Anything else makes us feel hurt, unloved and without consolation. We want absolute love, goodness, beauty and truth, to come to us and reveal itself absolutely and in a way that is epistemically and empirically undeniable.

Father Michael tells the following story from his time in seminary when he heard a lesson and then observed a pupil's response:

In every culture, in every society, in every family throughout
history, people like to tell and listen to stories, but nobody likes a
story without a point, and we love happy endings. That's because

153

we all recognise deep inside that our lives are both gift and task, the task being that we are called to make our lives into good stories! That is, they should have a point to them, and we want them to have a happy ending. The way our lives become good stories and have happy endings is by doing God's will. God has a plan for our lives, there's a specific way that He wants us to bring all of creation back to himself, and our happiness comes from helping him to do this according to our gifts and talents and in the way he wills for us. One of the students, an unbeliever who heard Fr Clarke speak this way, raised her hand and gave a remarkable response: Father, this makes sense and painful sense. I don't feel that my life is a good story. Instead, it's more like the sitcoms I watch on TV. They're just a series of episodes. There's no real point to them as a whole. They just go from one stupid joke to another with no end in mind. That's my life and the life of so many of my friends: We just go from one weekend to weekend, doing our best to have "fun" so as to avoid the gnawing, inner ache of a hidden desperation. But you're right. There is indeed something else inside me that's crying out, "Make your life a good story!" And in my own small way, I want to help the cosmos return to its source. (Gaitley 2012)

So perhaps in all this, Tom Bombadil is the vision of the being that returns the cosmos to its source. But is he really out there? I pointed Joost to the bi-location of Padre Pio, to the miracle of the Tilma of Guadalupe, and to the miracles of the Eucharist where the bread and wine literally become flesh and blood. What is the point of these miracles, and how do they relate to Tom Bombadil? I think it comes down to perception and reality. Jesus says, in Old English:

Ge synd middangeardes leoht – [You are the light of middle earth].
(Matthew 5)

This means that as members of the Body of Christ, a true miracle happens of transformation of creation, and therein we are returned to the Source of the Father, through the Holy Spirit, and we become fully into communion with the deepest reality. The whole cosmos refines its harmony and communion with us, and with the order of the angels too. This is an Incarnate reality, as human beings are a bridge between the Heavens and Matter, that is fulfilled in a Person - Jesus Christ - who leaves his Holy Spirit to be with his followers even until the end of time (Matthew 28), and who comes to us within the deepest yearnings of our own story.

The harmony and the dance of this communion of Peace, between us and this Person, brings forth a light that shines through Middle-earth as a resonant interplay between ecstasy and communion. The Incarnation and Resurrection brings forth a song of ecstasy, and as the Franciscans such as Duns Scotus have argued, the Incarnation fulfils God's desire to pour forth His love super-abundantly, which is the Good News of the Kingdom, which was an outpouring (they argue) that was not just a "rescue mission" in response to the Fall and Original Sin but rather an eternal desire to unite God and the cosmos through a man and his mystical marriage to his bride in a total harmony. *Tom Bombadil's joy in his marriage with Goldberry is interwoven within this Cosmic Narrative.*

I have always delighted in the Franciscan Romanticism of the Incarnation. God has such burning love for us, that from the first moment of Creation, Duns believed, God knew He must incarnate himself as Emmanuel, that is, to be 'God-with-us'. God planned this in order to unite himself more deeply with his creatures, irrespective, Scotus argued, of whether any of us would ever use our free will to sin. The Incarnation of Christ, on this standard Catholic view, is therefore not a 'divine rescue mission' hatched on a whim over humanity's Fall into sin, akin to the adventures of pagan deities like Perseus, the son of Zeus, saving the island of Seriphos. Rather, the Incarnation was the logical culmination of the Divine Reason built into the foundation of reality, out of Love. This also explains why Jesus was able to preach 'the Good News' before he died on the Cross, because that news is not merely his atoning death, as supposed by popular Reformed/Evangelical Christianity, but is primarily the mystical union of God and humanity achieved through Christ. None of this means that the Cross of Christ, his crucifixion, is not important for Eastern and Catholic Christians – far from it. The interpretation herein is from a Christian perspective but provides a meaningful way for non-Christians to think about the Cross also. When I talk about sin, I am not talking about anything shameful like a stain upon a person, but merely the absence of harmony with God's life living in us, and actions which bring such disharmony.

The Gospels are clear that Jesus saw his death on the Cross like a new Passover, the Jewish festival of deliverance from oppression. In this model Jesus is understood as the Passover lamb, sacrificed in obedience to God the Father, transformed for the liberation of God's people, a shared feast of God's gifts. The sacrifice of the Cross is efficacious for our salvation because it is Jesus completing the work of his incarnation by sharing in our death and hence fully uniting himself with humanity. This means that we, joined to the cosmic body of Christ, will not die in sin, but through his resurrection will share with him in the life of God. Christ here does not merely take our place as a substitute, but participates in us – as we do in him. Hence, Jesus' blood is spilled for us, not as a vindictive punishment or a human sacrifice to appease God's anger, but as the sharing of his divine lifeblood with us (Hardy 2020). So, what does "Bombadilic" harmony feel like in the Jewish experience and yearning? The following reference from Isaiah may clarify:

As the rain and the snow come down from Heaven, and do not return to it without watering the earth and making it bud and flourish, so that it yields seed for the sower and bread for the eater, so is my word that goes out from my mouth: It will not return to me empty, but will accomplish what I desire and achieve the purpose for which I sent it. You will go out in joy and be led forth

157

in peace; the mountains and hills will burst into song before you, and all the trees of the field will clap their hands. Instead of the thornbush will grow the juniper, and instead of briers the myrtle will grow. This will be for the Lord's renown, for an everlasting sign, that will endure forever. (Isaiah 55:10-14)

And as Tolkien writes in his "sense" of how Tom Bombadil and Goldberry should be, and perhaps are:

Old Tom Bombadil had a merry wedding,

crowned all with buttercups, hat and feather shedding;

his bride with forget me nots and flag-lilies for garland

was robed all in silver-green. He sang like a starling,

hummed like a honey-bee, lilted to the fiddle,

clasping his river-maid round her slender middle.

Lamps gleamed within his house, and white was the bedding;

in the bright honey-moon Badger-folk came treading,

danced down under Hill, and Old Man Willow

tapped, tapped at window-pane, as they slept on the pillow,

on the bank in the reeds River-woman sighing

heard Barrow-wight in his mound crying.

Old Tom Bombadil heeded not the voices,

taps, knocks, dancing feet, all the nightly noises;

slept till the sun arose, then sang like a starling:

'Hey! Come derry-dol, merry-dol, my darling!'

sitting on the door-step chopping sticks of willow,

158

while fair Goldberry combed her tresses yellow. (Tolkien 1962)

As Easter comes with her song each year, let us believe in the vision of cosmic harmony that Tolkien sensed and that Joost is searching for an "empirical verification" of. I commend Joost - he has inspired me. I am delighted in his sincerity. It is with this sincerity that we should be welcomed in turn to encounter the Spirit and Person of Tom Bombadil and Goldberry in the reality of our world and cosmos, and in turn be welcomed by them to receive the seven gifts of the Holy Spirit. It reminds me of Thomas the Apostle:

Now Thomas (also known as Didymus), one of the Twelve, was not with the disciples when Jesus came. So, the other disciples told him, "We have seen the Lord!" But he said to them, "Unless I see the nail marks in his hands and put my finger where the nails were, and put my hand into his side, I will not believe." A week later his disciples were in the house again, and Thomas was with them. Though the doors were locked, Jesus came and stood among them and said, "Peace be with you!" Then he said to Thomas, "Put your finger here; see my hands. Reach out your hand and put it into my side. Stop doubting and believe." Thomas said to him, "My Lord and my God!" Then Jesus told him, "Because you have seen me, you have believed; blessed are those who have not seen and yet have believed." (John 20:24-29)

CHAPTER 8:

The Dynamic Power of Transcendent Communion

om Bombadil and Goldberry are an enigma, so much so that Peter Jackson left them out of his movies (Jackson 2001-2003). So, *who* are they? Michael Organ has argued convincingly through his biographical analysis of Tolkien's narrative structuring, and also evidence from the evolution of the characters in his imagination as seen through his biography and letter writing, that Tom *is* the Holy Spirit, whilst also touching on the question of: Who then is Goldberry? He has reached this view not from a faith perspective, though he was brought up in the Roman Catholic tradition and thus has a familiarity with its spiritual landscape. I have been inspired by Michael's intuition and the recent scope of the documentary *Finding Tom Bombadil* which argues that Tom Bombadil was "not created but sensed" and follows the quest of Joost van de Loo, to find convincing empirical evidence for Tom's presence on our earth (van de Loo 2019a). These efforts have led me to take the question of Tom Bombadil more seriously. Through this ongoing conversation, it seems that Michael also agrees that Goldberry is of the "same substance" as Goldberry (to borrow a term from Theology). In essence, whatever they *are, they both are, and fully*. One is not more or less than the other. Michael and I also agree that Tom and Goldberry inhabit an a-temporal plane and provide a refreshing encounter with those who enter an interpersonal communion with them. Michael notes how the gifts received by the hobbits in the "Bombadil boot camp" episode, gear them up with gifts akin to the charismatic seven gifts of the Holy Spirit from the Catholic Tradition (Organ, 2019). He also notes that the encounter accompanies dreams and vision that also lead the hobbits to gain the endurance, which later proves so powerful in overcoming the seemingly boundless evils of their subsequent journey through Middle-earth. Michael says that in Tolkien's writing process, Tom Bombadil whose name came from a family doll that was dropped down the toilet, became a personage in Tolkien's mind who was "known from the beginning," whilst other characters emerged through the ongoing writing process itself. Tom was always present to Tolkien throughout, yet from the beginning (Organ, 2019).

I agreed with Michael's analysis based on an intuition which I seem to have carried since first having encountered Tom and Goldberry, an encounter that has marked me deeply and permeates me through an enigma that seems beyond the text; an invitation into something deeper. I first "met them" just before my English creative writing General Certificate of Education at the age of 16. I read those chapters in *The Lord of the Rings* as if for the "first time" and remember being filled with a numinous "sense" that remains with me to this day. I remember "knowing" that what was "right" was therein contained in Tolkien's words. I could not tell you why or how I knew but I had a "sense" that remains with me to this day. It was like a new knowledge, but also like a memory and a dream and a vision all at the same time, and filled with yearning; I knew I could find it, or at least seek that which was beyond!

This enigmatic quality of whatever Tom and Goldberry *are*, contributed to why Peter Jackson wanted to avoid representation. In doing so, it seems both the narrative mechanics and dynamics of Tolkien's story are changed in a way that is perhaps beyond recognition to the original. Michael makes the point clearly and I agree with him. Tom and Goldberry provide a causal-strength that provides the spiritual context of the hobbits' subsequent victory through endurance. Taking them out is like removing the "womb" from which the later "fruitfulness" of their spiritual endurance begins in those chapters in an embryonic potential form. In the three chapters, the potential of the totality is conceived and also seemingly held.

Julian of Norwich talks about such a mystical moment or encounter with infinity and had no idea her writings would bear fruit seven centuries later. She describes it in her *Revelations of Divine Love* as:

... seeing God holding a tiny thing in his hand, like a small brown nut, which seemed so fragile and insignificant that she wondered why it did not crumble before her eyes. She understood that the thing was the entire created universe, which is as nothing compared to its Creator, and she was told, 'God made it, God loves it, God keeps it.' (Julian of Norwich 1998)

Tolkien had a similar experience in vision of "infinite embrace" one day in Adoration of the Blessed Sacrament in his local parish. The Logos (Greek for divine reason) which is God's Word, is inseparable from God's Spirit, and flows forth from the Father. This Word was known to the Jewish world as Divine Wisdom, and it is this Word that is made incarnate in the historical Person of Jesus Christ. The Word is that of the Father, as Jesus taught:

Anyone who loves me will obey my teaching. My Father will love them, and we will come to them and make our home with them. (John 14:23)

Therein, where the Spirit dwells, the Father and the Word are also there in their fullness. It is this teaching that explains why in the Eucharistic Bread or Blessed Sacrament the consecration to the Holy Spirit of Host brings forth the fullness of the Divine Presence

164

in the gifts of bread and wine. An unveiling occurs within which the Trinity is revealed. What was previously known in the Jewish tradition as the Shekinah Glory, the presence of Adonai the God of Israel in the Holy of Holies, has now been fully revealed in the Eucharist, so that the barrier between the human and the Divine has been broken down, and divinisation is now made possible. As Tolkien remembered:

I perceived or thought of the Light of God and in it suspended one small mote (or millions of motes to only one of which was my small mind directed), glittering white because of the individual ray from the Light which both held and lit it…And the ray was the Guardian Angel of the mote: not a thing interposed between God and the creature, but God's very attention itself, personalized…This is a finite parallel to the Infinite. As the love of the Father and Son (who are infinite and equal) is a Person, so the love and attention of the Light to the Mote is a person (that is both with us and in Heaven): finite but divine, i.e., angelic." (Letter 60)

We stand then as receivers of Tolkien's illumined vision and sub-creation within an oral tradition that he received as gift and inspiration, and whose roots he saw as going back to the dawn of time in the Logos. Like Gandalf, who is originally unable to fully comprehend Tom Bombadil's significance at the Council of Elrond, as he is concerned with a temporal and martial victory over evil, we need to "see" things differently. After his transfiguration as "servant of the Secret Fire" into Gandalf the White, he returns

165

to the House of Tom Bombadil to speak to the "Master" once the Ring of Power is destroyed. This shows his path into communion and understanding with a Spirit, that seems more akin to the one known to the Prophet Elijah, who finds his Master in the "still small voice" beyond cosmic catastrophe and the dissonance of a fallen world:

The Lord said, "Go out and stand on the mountain in the presence of the Lord, for the Lord is about to pass by." Then a great and powerful wind tore the mountains apart and shattered the rocks before the Lord, but the Lord was not in the wind. After the wind there was an earthquake, but the Lord was not in the earthquake. After the earthquake came a fire, but the Lord was not in the fire. And after the fire came a gentle whisper." (1 Kings 19:11)

The gentle whisper is the way of Tom Bombadil and Goldberry. Their very being seems to be even beyond prelapsarian innocence or the glorification and divinisation of the human person in the traditions of the sacramental worldview; they are in a timeless affinity which is experienced in time by those who come into their presence and relate to them.

Three images from the history of art are noteworthy, in my opinion, as parallels to a transcendent and dynamic interpersonal communion, which is experienced "in time" in Middle-earth - at least a special mysterious kind of eternally-infused time - as encountered by the hobbits in the mystery of Tom Bombadil and

Goldberry in Arda. There are many more than these in the Biblical tradition, such as Abraham's three guests and the conjugal bliss of the Songs of Songs, or the New Jerusalem as Bride coming down from Heaven, and conventional fidelity as bridal. In fact, it seems an almost relentless image of the infused biblical imagination!

Firstly, in the Jewish tradition, within the Holy of Holies where the Shekinah is filled with the Divine Presence, there dwelt two seraphic angels who were the closest to the glory of God and His Mercy Seat (Hebrew 9:5). They were carved in an anticipatory ecstatic intercommunion and verge on embrace with each other in the presence of the Divinity. This was the highest artistic expression of the relationship of the Divinity to Israel. This tradition expresses that we reach the Divine Communion through the image of the anticipatory embrace of the cherubim angels. This is the sacral, dynamic and the most appropriate way to pass into the Mysteries. What is important is to note the exstasis (ex – out of / stasis – movement) of the communion; each angel fully in the process of being given to the other in a constant dialogue of praise.

The second image is possibly the most famous representation of the Trinity - the Rublev icon. In this sacral painting, we are invited into a tri-personal gaze that expresses the mystery of a Life-Giving communion, that is the Genesis of human inter-personality and is the finality of all human desire when "God will be All-in-All" through Love. This is all at once encounter and beatific vision. We encounter a Presence beyond the veil of the sacral painting.

Andrei Rublev, The Trinity, icon, 1360.

Thirdly, in the Jewish scriptures, Divine Wisdom takes the form of a feminine dancer at the dawn of Creation who leaps with rapture and ecstasy at the dawn of time in the presence of the "Master" (Proverbs 2:22-25). This Divine Feminine Wisdom is beautifully envisioned in the tapestry at Notre Dame Church in Central London. Divine Wisdom is fully innocent, blissful as the dappled dawn and filled with vigour and hope; mirroring with Grace, the boundless enthusiasms of the Master.

Dom Robert Ombelles, Divine *Wisdom as Bride, or the Blessed Virgin Mary as Immaculate Conception*, tapestry, Notre Dame Church, London, 1954.

The tapestry reads: *Cum eo eram cuncta componens ludens coram eo omni tempore / [I was by his side, like a master craftsman, ever at play in his presence]*

As Saint Maximillian Koble noted:

Mary is the created Immaculate Conception who is wedded to the uncreated Immaculate Conception; so that when she reveals who she IS - "I am the Immaculate Conception"- to the peasant girl Saint Bernadette, it is her and the Holy Spirit speaking as one and revealing their identity as being entwined. (Academy of the Immaculate 2004)

In these images we see life that is akin to Tom and Goldberry; a vitality, overflowing joy, and beauty in "spousal" (by analogy) inter-personality that invites communion and enlightenment, visions and dream sequences; through the experience of their hospitable benefaction or tremendous yet simple presence and gaze, speech and song.

Dom Robert Ombelles, *God in his "carpet slippers" creating Man*, [extract], France Today, 2017.

As Michael has noted, Tom Bombadil is "Fatherless" and in this sense makes himself akin or one with the True Father, who Chesterton notes paradoxically is "younger than we" (Chesterton, 1908). Boundless vitality in Tom and Goldberry, imbibes the hobbits with strength to fulfil their narratival destiny. They find the strength to understand their story and carry it out, despite their littleness; after being drawn into the communion.

The argument of postmodernity is that there is infinite perception and no "true story" beyond this, only interpretation. Tom and Goldberry seem to invite an enigma of the same standard as the postmodern criticism of epistemology. Tom is overwhelmed by his relationship to Goldberry, who brings him tumbling to the bottom of the river, and in being His "Wife" is a person of infinite perceptive value, playful and life-giving reciprocity of Light; totally free. Is this not what postmodernity wants, *but* more? She is also the one who receives and dialogues with the outpouring of His song and devotion, knowing His very nature, as Logos, that "He is." This post-modern infinite playfulness *is in communion with Logos,* not opposed to it; but of one Spirit!

As Father Michael Gaitley has shown, the Trinity is an invitation into interpersonal love, not just looking at two people who love each other at a marriage, but more to "be" the child of their marriage who receives their love and is the personal fruit of their love. In this sense every "birth" of a child gives continuous glory to the transcendent interpersonal communion of the Trinity, by the coming into being of "new tri-personal" communion from the nuptial ecstasy and unity of man and woman bringing new personal life into relational being. This analogy should not be "read back into the Trinity" in a way that demystifies a mystery, but it is

171

consistently an icon of the Divine Life from the Judaeo-Christian mystical tradition, arguably best typified by the Song of Songs that became a favourite for spiritual exegesis in the medieval tradition, thus engendering spiritual fecundity of the "child" of God who ponders the mystery of the Lover-Beloved, in relation to it actively and dynamically, and thereby finds "food" for a spiritually fruitful contemplative engagement within the world. The mystery has an apex case for the Catholic mind, in the virginal fruitfulness of the chaste and adoptive Saint Joseph and the Immaculate Mother of God who sheltered and raised the Logos-man. In any case my argument is that tri-fold interpersonality occurs and "invites us" in the Spirit that exists through the hobbits (our bridge into the Story) who bring "us" into a relational encounter with Tom and Goldberry, where we end up being caught within the Spirit of their relation to each other. Truly an enchanting (en-chanson; in a song) and dream-inspiring eternal moment in time.

What the Jews call Covenant was a temple in time where God outpoured His Presence to the faithful Jew as communion, and what the New and Eternal Covenant experienced by the Catholic disciple calls Sacramental Communion, where a veil is lifted and the faithful are brought into Trinitarian Communion through their bodily receipt of the Divine and mystical gifts. Tolkien said the one thing on earth to "adore" was the Blessed Sacrament, as it grants "eternal endurance to earthly love." He seems to invite his reader into the rapture of the life-giving experience of the dynamics of ecstatic Adoration through meeting Tom and Goldberry. His familiarity with the structure of the mystical experience seems to seep into his writing and consolidate the effect. It remains known-enigma to Tolkien, not as a Gnostic secret but as the mystery of eternal-sacrament, experienced in every Tabernacle of the earth by the Catholic faithful drawn into that Love.

A person in the presence of Tom and Goldberry is seized by the Spirit that exists between them, that captures any person who meets them, which is and of itself IS a person: 1) Tom - fatherless Master/Logos who can speak to the creation with authority, like God in the garden of Eden from Genesis 2, who strolls beside humanity in intimacy; 2) Goldberry – Divine Wisdom that dances in the presence of the Master; and 3) in total freedom of Spirit.

The mystery of the Tri-fold communion of person "Father, Son and Holy Spirit" are such that each person is fully in the other and through the other. This is known as perichoresis. As has been shown above, this perichoretic ecstasy passes through the "types" and "icons" of interpersonal and nuptial ecstasy in Judeo-Christianity.

The same hobbits who we are "living through" narratively within *The Lord of the Rings* are imbued with spiritual gifts for their impending battle through Middle-earth. It is through their encounter as persons, with the persons of Tom and Goldberry and entering by hospitality into the Spirit of their relation, that the hobbits are able to do what they then do. Tom and Goldberry are a crux in the narrative, that is like a "womb" of the later success. To take them out is *to miss the essential as it is so subtle*. Perhaps that is what Gandalf was wrestling with at the Council of Elrond, when considering Tom's purposes for the future of the Ring of Power, and then leaving him out of the plan.

I am not arguing that this is a strict exegesis to be read as such. Tolkien's letters when questioned regarding the nature of Bombadil show a playful joy that disguises his biographical and existential familiarity with Tom, in enigma, that in turn invites his correspondent into the mystery. In September 1954, in his letter to Peter Hastings, the Professor is playfully enigmatic (Letter 153). The statements therein could be understood in the context of Tolkien's comment about the first layer of his writing being pregnant with a latent "unconscious" Catholicism, as his work is "fundamentally religious" in nature, but by a later "conscious by revision" (Letter 142).

For Tolkien, who was passionate about the Logos in his relentlessly fruitful zeal for philological Wisdom, it is no surprise that the mystery of the Trinity, the enigma within the story of his own life, should play a definitive role in his narrative. There was also an absolute subtlety in the handling of the One who "is", though perhaps this was done totally unconsciously. It still, however, continues to provide an enigmatic invitation. Are Tom

174

and Goldberry the crux and apex case of the enigmatic Presence "known" to Tolkien and that suffused his imagination with illumination, and all at once a concealed and revealed spiritually refreshing mystery that even Peter Jackson had to leave out because it was too intriguingly simple? Was Tolkien seeking: *To give subtilty to the simple, to the young man knowledge and discretion* (Proverbs 1:4)?

CHAPTER 9:

The Kenosis of the Secret Fire as the Metaphysical Foundation of the Freedom of Tom and Goldberry

"No time for it," said the wizard. "But—," said Bilbo again. "No time for that either! Off you go!" To the end of his days Bilbo could never remember how he found himself outside, without a hat, a walking-stick or any money, or anything that he usually took when he went out; leaving his second breakfast half-finished and quite unwashed-up, pushing his keys into Gandalf's hands, and running as fast as his furry feet could carry him down the lane, past the great Mill, across The Water, and then on for a mile or more"

– The Hobbit, Chapter 2

Gandalf closes his eyes as he hears Frodo's statement. The members of the council slowly turn towards Frodo, astonished. Frodo: "I will take the Ring to Mordor. Though — I do not know the way."

– The Fellowship of the Ring, Peter Jackson

The urgency of vocation and the call of beauty to personal kenosis

vocation (n.) early 15c., "spiritual calling," from Old French vocacion "call, consecration; calling, profession" (13c.) or directly from Latin vocationem (nominative vocatio), literally "a calling, a being called" from vocatus "called," past participle of vocare "to call" (from PIE root *wekw- "to speak"). Sense of "one's occupation or profession" is first attested in the 1550s.

adventure (v.) c. 1300, aventuren, "to risk the loss of," from Old French aventurer (12c.) "wander, travel; seek adventure; happen by chance," from aventure (n.); see adventure (n.). Meaning "take a chance" is early 14c. Related: Adventured; adventuring.

The link between good and beautiful stirs fruitful reflection. In a certain sense, beauty is the visible form of the good, just as the good is the metaphysical condition of beauty. This was well understood by the Greeks who, by fusing the two concepts, coined a term which embraces both: *kalokagathía*, or beauty-goodness. On this point Plato writes:

The power of the Good has taken refuge in the nature of the Beautiful. (John Paul II, 1999)

The word *kalon* is the name of naming: it names that which, in speech, calls. When applied reflexively and responsorially to its own origin, which here is the origin of all proper denomination, it

178

designates its power. Beautiful, *kalon*, is what comes from a call, *kalein*, which continues to call through it and in it. *Kalein* possesses in Greek the same double meaning that "to call" has in French, at once to call out, hail, summon, and to bestow a name, to name (Chrétien 2004). Or, as Gerard Manley Hopkins put it in his poem *As Kingfishers Catch Fire*:

Each mortal thing does one thing and the same:

Deals out that being indoors each one dwells;

Selves — goes itself; *myself* it speaks and spells,

Crying *Whát I dó is me: for that I came.* (Hopkins 1985)

Kenosis is Christian life. It means to become outpouring. It means to become a total gift and a radical gift. To achieve kenosis a Christian must be brought to a position of total surrender and total obedience to the Divine Will, seeking nothing but to give all that they are to the work that God has entrusted them to do. Kenosis is the deepest theological drama and truth of the human heart, which transcends the creation of the world and is prior to it but incarnate in the crucified heart of Jesus, which was enfleshed by Mary's total self-surrender of her body until death.

Now on earth there exists a new Tabernacle in time which is the heart of the human person where the Secret Fire dwells. The Secret Fire is that love which exists as outpouring in God who is communion. God is total risk and total abandonment in his eternal being. In God we have the openness of all love, which embraces the polarities of agony and ecstasy that historically manifest themselves in the narrative of divine solidarity, crucifixion and resurrection in the life of Jesus of Nazareth. In Letter to the Philippians, we read:

Therefore, if you have any encouragement from being united with Christ, if any comfort from his love, if any common sharing in the Spirit, if any tenderness and compassion, then make my joy complete by being like-minded, having the same love, being one in spirit and of one mind. Do nothing out of selfish ambition or vain conceit. Rather, in humility value others above yourselves, not looking to your own interests but each of you to the interests of the others. (Philippians 2:1-4)

In your relationships with one another, have the same mindset as Christ Jesus:

Who, being in very nature God, did not consider equality with God something to be used to his own advantage; rather, he made himself nothing by taking the very nature of a servant, being made in human likeness.

In Christian theology, kenosis (Greek: κένωσις, kénōsis, lit. [the act of emptying]) is the 'self-emptying' of Jesus' own will and becoming entirely receptive to God's divine will. The word ἐκένωσεν (ekénōsen) is used in Philippians 2:7, "[Jesus] made himself nothing …")

And being found in appearance as a man, he humbled himself by becoming obedient to death — even death on a cross!

Humiliate can be traced back to the Latin humus, meaning "earth, ground." From humus came the Latin adjective humilis, meaning "low, humble," which later gave rise to the verb humiliare, meaning "to make low or humble." The English humiliate derives from Latin humiliare.

Therefore, God exalted him to the highest place and gave him the name that is above every name, that at the name of Jesus every knee should bow, in Heaven and on earth and under the earth, and every tongue acknowledge that Jesus Christ is Lord, to the glory of God the Father (Philippians 2:1-11).

This is the theodramatic structure that von Balthasar senses and intuits and is the basis of all Christian vocation (Zuidervaart 2013). To be a Christian is to willingly surrender to the obedience of humiliation, which brings our very flesh into true correspondence with reality as God comes to dwell in each human soul as the Trinity of Secret Fire – that which kindles eternal life in each person through the deepest purgation. To allow the possibility of such a transformation only one thing is necessary: that before God a Christian surrenders all that they are and all that they hope to be. This is the structure of death as divine paradox that J.R.R. Tolkien intuited when he notes on the Blessed Sacrament that it gives life and eternal endurance to all human loves, as its ontological status is total oblation of self and total outpouring (Kreeft, 2005)

For Von Balthasar the Trinitarian outpouring as kenosis, is found in the Logos that proceeds from the Father and Holy Spirit and is the source of the inner radiance and light of all of the created world. For Balthasar, The Logos is the basis of meaning, as the whole created order is orientated to the return to Father, through the Logos or Son (Polanco 2017). As Von Balthasar writes, even though the creation and its creatures run from the Father, they run away *into the Son* and this is the drama of human history, which is the outplaying of a dramatic history of freedom; to love or not love, to be or not to be.

As William Shakespeare has noted: "to be or not to be, that is the question." [* "To be, or not to be" is the opening phrase of a soliloquy spoken by Prince Hamlet in the so-called "nunnery scene" of William Shakespeare's play Hamlet. Act III, Scene I.] Shall we love or shall we not love? – the whole salvation of the flesh and the spirit is hinged on this radical choice that is grounded historically in the freedom of every human life and the struggle of its soul. Love is the greatest adventure; it is the great exodus outside of the self as Pope Francis has noted in two important statements. The first:

To offer one's life in mission is possible only if we are able to leave ourselves behind. On this 52nd World Day of Prayer for Vocations,

I would like to reflect on that particular "exodus" which is the heart of vocation, or better yet, of our response to the vocation God gives us. When we hear the word "exodus", we immediately think of the origins of the amazing love story between God and his people, a history which passes through the dramatic period of slavery in Egypt, the calling of Moses, the experience of liberation and the journey toward the Promised Land. (Pope Francis, 2015)

The second:

In the context of contemporary literature, J.R.R. Tolkien's characters Bilbo and Frodo recover the image of a man (human) who is called to walk. The author's heroes know and operate, in walking, the dramatic struggle between good and evil. The "man on the way" (or, The Man as wayfarer") implies a dimension of hope – crossing the threshold of hope. Every story and human mythology underscores that man is not a static or halted being but rather "on the way", called, "vocated" (hence the word vocation). When man does not enter this dynamic, he is nullified or decays as a person. (Bergoglio, 2008)

In each human soul there is a wealth and richness of life, a landscape no smaller in nobility and possibility than all the realms and opportunities of Middle-Earth. Responding to God's unique adventure of vocation to each person, is the greatest quest of every human soul – and demands the risk of their whole life and being:

The decision to go away from Christ was definitively influenced only by external riches, what the young man possessed ("possessions"). Not by what he was! What he was, as precisely a young man - the interior treasure hidden in youth - had led him to Jesus. And it had also impelled him to ask those questions which in the clearest way concern the plan for the whole of life. What must I do? "What must I do to inherit eternal life?" What must I do so that my life may have full value and full meaning? The youth of each one of you, dear friends, is a treasure that is manifested precisely in these questions. Man asks himself these questions throughout his life. But in the time of youth they are particularly urgent, indeed insistent. And it is good that this is so. (John Paul II 1985)

In Frodo's submission or fiat to take the ring to Mordor, which parallels his uncle Bilbo's ecstatic venture out of Hobbiton to defeat a dragon and regain a long-forgotten treasure hoard, at the peril of losing his whole life, we see the type of all Christian vocation and narrative. When Frodo says "I will take the ring to Mordor – though I do not know the way," we see a hobbit animated by a Secret Fire, by a secret intuition about the structure of reality and the need for total surrender to fulfil the deepest desires of the heart. Both Frodo and Bilbo have been called to death and in moments of profound drama, they have sensed with urgency that the surrender of all their hopes, dreams and desires for a normal life uninterrupted by episodes of peril, chaos, violence, despair, agony and ecstasy, will be shattered if they answer with the obedience necessary to continue along pathways that have been opened to them by "luck"; that Providential undertone which colours the structural reality of the stories of Middle-earth. Joining Frodo and Bilbo are many other characters who are to be tested in the Secret Fire. This is the mystery of the Divine folly of love that calls all to enter into the paradox of power latent to kenosis; that to gain all one must give all… *and is this not epitomised in the freedom of Tom Bombadil and Goldberry at their negation of the ring… do they not all at once express the freedom of kenosis as the revelation of the transcendent freedom of the Holy Spirit which is the origin and destiny of the human person?*

All those within the Lord of Rings who want to reach and acquire this Divine Life and Spirit must enter into a pathway of purgation:

O LORD, thou hast seduced me, and I was seduced; thou wert stronger than I and hast overcome me; I am in derision daily; everyone mocks me. For since I spoke out, I raised my voice crying, violence and destruction; because the word of the LORD has been a reproach unto me and a derision, daily. And I said, I will not make mention of him, nor speak any more in his name. But he was in my heart as a burning fire and within my bones; I tried to forbear, and I could not. (Jeremiah 20:7-9)

Similarly:

185

Gold is tested by fire, and human character is tested in the furnace of humiliation. Trust the Lord, and he will help you. Walk straight in his ways, and put your hope in him. All you that fear the Lord, wait for him to show you his mercy. Do not turn away from him, or you will fall. (Sirach 2:5-7)

Aragorn too senses a deep call that has marked his whole life and to which he has been estranged, roaming wildly in woods and wandering along hidden pathways. But he too must tread the paths of the dead to return as King and Master of himself and thus of the whole Kingdom that has been entrusted to his care. Woven more deeply into the fibres of Middle-earth as a narratival reality, we also find Luthien who pours out her immortal life for love of Beren:

Here we meet, among other things, the first policies of world history. 'The wheels of the world', are often turned not by the Lords and Governors, even gods, but by the seemingly unknown and weak – owing to the secret life in creation, and the part unknowable to all wisdom but One, that resides in the intrusions of the Children of God into the Drama. (Letter 131)

In the location of Frodo's spiritual agony, in which he is pierced by the evil of Middle-earth on Weathertop, we have a juxtaposition in Strider's (Aragorn) preceding tale of total gift and outpouring in the love of Luthien. This will be mirrored in the love of Arwen for Aragorn, who also makes the gift of her immortal life for love of him:

A gift I will give you. For I am the daughter of Elrond. I shall not go with him now when he departs to the Havens; for mine is the choice of Lúthien, and as she so have I chosen, both the sweet and the bitter. But in my stead you shall go, Ring-bearer, when the time comes, and if you then desire it. If your hurts grieve you still and the memory of your burden is heavy, then you may pass into the West, until all your wounds and weariness are healed. (LOTR)

Continually we find that the theodrama of Middle-earth is the theodrama of kenosis and this is what elevates Tolkien's tale into the Divine Imagination of the Secret Fire (von Balthasar 1993). This Secret Fire was longed for by Melkor, but he refused the ontological structure of gift and became a discordant rebel. The dissonance of Melkor is what has plagued Middle-earth's history with evil and the absence of radiance or correspondence to the structure of reality. According to Tolkien's mythological creation story of Middle-earth, the *Ainulindalë*:

To Melkor among the Ainur had been given the greatest gifts of power and knowledge, and he had a share in all the gifts of his brethren; and he had gone often alone into the void places seeking the Imperishable Flame. For desire grew hot within him to bring into Being things of his own, and it seemed to him that Ilúvatar took no thought for the Void, and he was impatient of its emptiness.

Yet he found not the Fire, for it is with Ilúvatar. But being alone he had begun to conceive thoughts of his own unlike those of his brethren. Some of these thoughts he now wove into his music, and straightway discord arose about him, and many that sang nigh him grew despondent, and their thought was disturbed and their music faltered; but some began to attune their music to his rather than to the thought which they had at first. Then the discord of Melkor spread ever wider, and the melodies which had been heard at first foundered in a sea of turbulent sound. But Ilúvatar sat and hearkened until it seemed that about his throne there was a raging storm, as of dark waters that made war one upon the other in an endless wrath that would not be assuaged. Then Ilúvatar arose, and the Ainur perceived that he smiled; and he lifted up his left hand, and a new theme began amid the storm, like and yet unlike to the former theme, and it gathered power and had new beauty. But the discord of Melkor rose in uproar and contended with it, and there was again a war of sound more violent than before, until many of the Ainur were dismayed and played no longer, and Melkor had the mastery. Then again Ilúvatar arose, and the Ainur perceived that his countenance was stern; and he lifted up his right hand; and behold, a third theme grew amid the confusion, and it was unlike the others. For it seemed at first soft and sweet, a mere rippling of gentle sounds in delicate melodies, but it could not be quenched, and it grew, and it took to itself power and profundity. And it seemed at last that there were two musics progressing at one time before the seat of Ilúvatar, and they were utterly at variance. One was deep and wide and beautiful, but slow and blended with an immeasurable sorrow, from which its beauty chiefly came. The other had now achieved a unity of its own; but it was loud, and vain, and endlessly repeated; and it had little harmony, but rather a clamorous unison as of many trumpets braying upon a few notes. And it essayed to drown the other music by the violence of its voice, but it seemed that its most triumphant notes were taken by the other and woven into its own solemn pattern. (Silmarillion)

Von Balthasar's mystic intuition informed by the visions of Adrian von Speyr and his love of classical music conforms beautifully with Tolkien's numinous sense that there is a song *deeper than all sorrow* that can weave discord into concord. This is the song of kenosis, or of Secret Fire (The Flame Imperishable), which purifies and removes all evil through the response of a God who has "smiled" upon the world and who is Divine love... *Epitomised so beautifully in the joyous and smiling hospitality of Tom Bombadil and Goldberry...* and abundance of joy which expresses the innocence, freedom and Grace of the Divine Spirit. However, Tolkien sensed this theodramatic music must be incarnated historically in the life and salvation of every human being, as a sacramental reality:

The "final word" on Beren and Lúthien is both harrowing and wonderful. It is the stuff, as Tolkien said, of "Joy beyond the walls of the world, poignant as grief." (Carswell 2017)

Tolkien's shared grave with his wife has upon the inscription of the lover's names Beren and Luthien, who *chose death to find life*. The structure and dynamism of kenosis underpins the whole narratival theodrama of Middle-earth and the heroism of their characters is found in the gift they make of themselves for the sake of a higher purpose to defend all that is good, beautiful and true. Kenosis is the most profound human desire and longing, and in Christian vocation can be fulfilled through responding to the vocation to oblation, of self-sacrifice, on the altar of one's own life. In marriage couples pledge their very flesh to each other in the ecstasy of a life-long communion that brings new life to the world. In the priesthood a man will die upon the altar each day to subordinate his earthly loves to the Divine love or Secret Fire that will purify the world of all evil. In religious life a Christian gives all that they are to become totally united and conformed to Christ in every moment through total praise. All Christian life is thus ultimately an entering into the kenosis of Christ – a humiliation and purgation that makes a human truly human and thus capable of the Divine… the pathway of Frodo is sustained by the dreams, visions and prophecies revealed to him in the house of Tom Bombadil and Goldberry, for the love of Christ has brought an inner structure of radiance and Grace to the whole created order, such that all creation can now be orientated to its true purpose. The humble can be ennobled as the Secret Fire operates to renew and sanctify all that has been made, to return to the goal of communion with God the Father, in this blazing spirit of renewal. This Secret

Fire is true and final authority against all the forces of discordance and evil. Indeed, Gandalf faces the demonic Balrog in Peter Jackson's adaptation of *The Lord of the Rings – The Fellowship of the Ring* with the words:

You cannot pass!…I am the servant of the Secret Fire, wielder of the Flame of Anor…The dark fire will not avail you! Flame of Udûn! Go back to the Shadow! You — shall not — pass!" (Jackson 2001)

Humiliation is the necessary prelude to glorification and the structure of this kenosis is found in the hobbits' quest to fight for the good, and is rightly celebrated in King Aragorn's final words to the hobbits: "You bow to no-one", as the renewed Kingdom will bow to the lowly and those who have allowed themselves to be purified by God. To be a Christian is to enter into the theodrama of reality, by willingly submitting to the purification of obedience to the Divine Will, which is love. Tolkien's narrative is one in which this structure of reality has been refined and enshrined through a fecund imagination that delights in the detail of beauty through narrative grounded in philological delight:

The Light of Valinor (derived from light before any fall) is the light of art undivorced from reason, that sees things both scientifically (or philosophically) and imaginatively (or sub-creatively) and 'says that they are good' – as beautiful (Letter 131)

The spiritual wealth of Tolkien's vision is ultimately Christocentric and grounded in a sacramental vision that is at once Eucharistic and Mariological. In the Blessed Sacrament, Tolkien sensed the radical self-gift of God to man, which gives life to all and meaning to all human love, as it is rightly-orientated to its true purpose and has undergone the purification of death.

Tolkien is considered a saint by some contemporary Catholics (Davis 2022). A saint is somebody who shares the "joys and the hopes, the griefs and the anxieties" of their generation and brings the presence of Christ to all as the Second Vatican Council document states (Lumen Gentium 1964). In Mary, Tolkien sensed that all beauty dwelt in simplicity and magnificence because she of all creatures was totally conformed to the Divine purpose. Bringing into the light this inner structure of radiance and ecstasy, is the life-force of the narrative of Middle-earth; *a life-force brought to the fore in the artistic and sacramental expression of the relationship of Tom and Goldberry who are totally given to each other in Love.* A deeper knowledge of the importance of the total gift of the self is renewed in Christian life such that each individual brings the light of their own personal vocation into being. Jordan Peterson has recently argued that Western Civilisation, grounded in the Logos, was what prevented tyranny. Peterson says that there is nothing better you can do than to transform into Logos aka shine a light on the whole world (Peterson, 2017). As one commentator learned from Peterson:

Within each of us is the potential to commit acts of great evil or be complicit in them, and that innocence is not the same as goodness, and we cannot know we are good until we do the right thing when the evil choice is easier. Religious narratives tend to highlight this transformational process, through which we better ourselves and repair our societies, and which provide us with ideal-archetypes we can emulate in our own journeys. Peterson believes we all must undertake this journey to have complete and fulfilled lives. (Parvulesco 2018)

The importance of the Logos was also noted in EWTN's documentary *Discovering Tolkien* when Dr David Howlett, who had personally met Tolkien, argues:

He was a colossal productive scholar, a philologist where Logos in Greek is a complicated word; indeed at the beginning of John's Gospel there is word and the word is Divine, and this was Tolkien's love. (EWTN 2018)

The response of kenosis to the Divinely inspired vocation of each individual, is that they bring a light that must not be hidden "under a bushel" (Matthew 5:15), that must blaze as Jesus himself said in the Saxon Gospels "*ge synd middangeardes leoht*" – "you are the light of middle earth" (Kemble 1858). Failing to enter into the structure of reality where the Secret Fire dwells in the gift of self, the world is left impoverished of you, of your personal light.

Agreeing with Peterson, the light of the individual and the theodrama of their own salvation, occurs precisely as they struggle to become capable of a love that is enshrined by Tolkien in the story of hobbits, little individuals caught up in tumultuous realties of a scope and scale that makes their own failures, escapades, trials and victories seem totally peripheral and insignificant. The opposite is true, in that the individual is totally important, and the person on pilgrimage to conform their life to the radiance of God's love, is the struggle that is at the core of all reality in the freedom of the will. A hobbit like Frodo, Sam or Bilbo in this way, is a human individual or a self-aware Christian in search of and responding personally to their vocation to love. The magnitude of individual quest shows the dignity of this call to kenosis for the sake of saving the whole world, in the mastery of one's own personal quest – which no other has been called to *but an individual personally.*

Western civilisation has long been fighting the long defeat – against the tyranny of Melchor that does not want things to be as they should be, for individuals to be as they should, as Eru had intended them:

He has dwelt in the West since the days of dawn, and I have dwelt with him years uncounted . . . and together through ages of the world we have fought the long defeat. - Lady Galadriel to Frodo (LOTR).

This was expanded upon by Tolkien outside of *The Lord of the Rings*:

I am a Christian, and indeed a Roman Catholic," he writes in one of his letters, "so that I do not expect 'history' to be anything but a 'long defeat'—though it contains (and in a legend may contain more clearly and movingly) some samples or glimpses of final victory. (Letter 195)

The nuptial faithfulness by analogy of human communion that prevents the falling into tyranny is described beautifully in Tolkien's vision of marital love:

The romantic chivalric tradition takes, or at any rate has in the past taken, the young man's eye off women as they are, as companions in shipwreck not guiding stars. (Letter 43)

So too in Aragorn's rally against the fall of civilisation in Peter Jackson's film adaptation of *The Lord of the Ring - The Return of the King*:

Sons of Gondor! Of Rohan! My brothers. I see in your eyes the same fear that would take the heart of me. (LOTR)

A day may come when the courage of Men fails, when we forsake our friends and break all bonds of fellowship, but it is not this day. An hour of wolves and shattered shields when the Age of Men comes crashing down, but it is not this day! This day we fight! By all that you hold dear on this good earth, I bid you stand, Men of the West! (Jackson 2003)

The freedom for which they stand is that of Tom Bombadil and Goldberry, *the radiance of their Spirit, the light that shuts out the night...* when all things are said and done, it is the illuminating joy of that couple's' Spirit which is the destiny of Middle-earth; beyond the darkness there is a beauty more ancient, and new, which sustains all Hope... *that is the Holy Spirit.*

CHAPTER 10:

The Goldberry Psyche

Epistemology, Self-Compassion and Liberating Love

Edmund Gettier (1927-2021) changed the course of modern philosophy and the theory of knowledge, known as epistemology, by unravelling the mystery of what actually constitutes knowledge. Gettier Cases have been used to show that knowledge is more than "justified true belief". After Gettier, the thousand-year-old tradition that knowing something involved having justification, i.e., the thing to be actually true and that you believed it, was no longer viable. Gettier had given the simple example of someone who hits a golf ball onto a green, sees it on the green and constructs the phrase "my golf ball is on the green." He arrives at the green but realises that he was looking at a similar golf ball belonging to someone else, whilst his golf ball, which was also on the green, is not the one he was looking at from afar. In this simple way the tradition was shown to be deficient. As Gettier demonstrates:

Various attempts have been made in recent years to state necessary and sufficient conditions for someone knowing a given proposition. The attempts have often been such that they can be stated in a form similar to the following: (a) S knows that P IFF (i.e., if and only if); (i) P is true, (ii) S believes that P, and (iii) S is justified in believing that P. (Gettier 1963)

Gettier shows that this knowledge is insufficient and reopens the epistemological adventure afresh with daring simplicity. The adventure highlights the limitations of having a theory of how we "know we know" anything. But this is surely not ethically a viable place to stay in our mind when we are faced with the inconceivable suffering of the world and our own life. This, in fact, leads us to a compassionate regard to ourselves and others, which staying simply in epistemological reflection cannot really lead us to ascertain. Though even this isn't enough, because we want to share our learning, and so we become philosophy-educators if we are brave, and wish to teach wisdom ("Philos - love" of "Sophia - wisdom"). But then even this is not enough, because sharing "knowledge of what to do with knowledge" is not actually doing it. So, the only thing that can take us more deeply towards what we want to communicate at this depth, is to become storytellers. That is, I could tell the following story if I wanted someone to gain wisdom about what a person should do:

"Are you a dead branch, who goes with the river... or are you alive, and struggling against the current and going back to the source, even if doing so will likely cost you everything, including your life?"

Or are you, as Tolkien suggests as a great story-teller himself:

You must choose, Beren, between these two: to relinquish the quest and your oath and seek a life of wandering upon the face of the earth; or to hold to your word and challenge the power of darkness upon its throne. But on either road, I shall go with you, and our doom shall be alike. (Silmarillion)

Holding true to your word is what Logos identifies in the Greek tradition as being "possessed by the truth" that goes beyond simply our reasoning, and that takes everything that we are into consideration. Logos can be defined in two specific contexts:

1. Theology – as the Word of God, or principle of divine reason and creative order, identified in the Gospel of John with the second person of the Trinity incarnate in Jesus Christ.

2. In Jungian psychology – as the principle of reason and judgement, associated with the animus.

When we approach the Logos with our whole lives, through our mind that governs our actions, as a response to the prayer of our soul, then we reach a sort of mysticism about what to do next, which is not a "not knowing" but simply a "not knowing how what we know, could actually come about to be known more." A mystic coming close to the Logos in this way, understands themself to be entering into the Logos' own story as they push their own mind to the limit. This would be, to take a mind-exercise, like the experience of finding out you belong at "home" in an imaginary kingdom where your deepest desires, purified by suffering, have been made into reality and which you enter into as a discovery of something totally new but also something that you already "knew"!

Tolkien's relationship with the Logos reached this sort of mysticism, as he was devoted to Saint John who taught that:

In the beginning was the Word, and the Word was with God, and the Word was God. (John 1:1)

Tolkien as a philo-logist (lover of words) was searching for the imprints of the transcendent Logos in the vestigial footprints of oral tradition and literature that pointed the direction to go back to the Source of all Truth. Searching for the Truth and allowing our mind to grasp it and the implications of our grasping it, is the purpose of psychology. Devoting your life to the journey of the soul in its reflection on a profound search for the Truth, there arguably emerges a pattern of purification by the Secret Fire that I have noted as something I would call the "Goldberry Psyche."

The Goldberry Psyche is a movement beyond a certain malady which itself contains the dynamism for the cure for re-establishing healthy relationships between two human beings in the affective, spiritual, mental, physical, psychological and erotic spheres of existence. It resorts to telling a story with the view that within telling this story, a psychological truth will be revealed that is beyond, but not exclusive of, epistemological knowledge; that is, we can know that we know it, even though we are not fully sure what it is that we know yet. It is also a truth that leads us to compassion towards ourselves and others and so brings forth wisdom. But if it is pure "psyche" (i.e., the human soul, mind, or spirit) then it will be contained within the Logos and flowing forth from it too at its Source. Because the Logos takes us beyond even philosophy in that its concern is religious (religare — Latin for "binding" or "unifying") it is able to hold together all knowledge (epistemology) and wisdom. All that suffering has borne fruit to teach us what is most important to know, and in this way the Logos nourishes the human mind the most. The Logos is the nourishment and healing of the mind, and so it is such for psyche-logoists (psychologists) who find the truth. Therefore, if the Goldberry Psyche could lead us into a contemplation of the Logos and the truth, what would it illuminate in us and what would we do about it? That is the concern of my theological poem, Into the Mystery, about the mystery of Tom Bombadil and Goldberry:

Into the mystery

His very being is turned to her

With Tom and Goldberry there

Goldberry is infinite playfulness and perception

Water's infinite spirited conversation

Reuniting the Logos (Eru)

through Tom Bombadil (Master of the Secret Fire)

… to the infinite playfulness of perception (Goldberry)

We are part of the continuation of this story through Tradition!

– eternal revolution –

Is in a tumbling River!

we are part of the eternal playfulness…within history…

Of something deeper than death; more innocent than sin

History is just one moment – Logos/mind

And Evangelisation is presence and innocence

All at once and "kind" (from "kin" by etymology)

sublime.

Goldberry – Tom

– interpersonal dynamic communion

… they're like a womb within Middle-earth that within

the hobbits find reunion

(an atemporal womb where they can dream)

and being empowered they can then go out

Tom and Goldberry – Master and Divine Wisdom dancing at the
dawn of creation

Ecstatic illumination and the Trinity-invitation Laden table
within the fable, but REAL. Connected to the Source;

Pilgrims can then perform the "Great Exorcism" of Middan Gard

Tom and Goldberry are timeless and entering time,

we via the hobbits are brought

into their fruitful interplay and communion

This reveals

a tri-fold interpersonal

communion

that breaks the boundaries

of the liminal realm of time and timelessness

Passing through the

types

of pre-lapsarian innocence

and transcendent sacramental perichoresis

… of which sacramental fruitfulness is the outpouring of A
Doorway into radiance

(we through the Theotokos,

stand in that communion

– Mary, "simplicity and magnificence"

– the knowledge about all beauty as Tolkien said.

Adam as catalogos – priest

and Christ as logos-priest

(the dynamism of exitus and reditus)

Bursting with innocence and new speech so ancient! Tom is not
in the martial-plane (the still silent voice, not at war with itself or
other) – hence at the council of Elrond, Gandalf is not sure of the
martial world (in the fallen world)

It's surely not the final voice, but the deepest innocence is greater
even than any martial victory (!),

… Source of the Transfigured Gandalf (who going into the a-
temporal Source,

then becomes fully-imbued with the White-Light of the Secret
Fire;

"servant" still but more?)

… that Well of transfiguring innocence is older than time and
transcends creation, it's a life-giving ecstasy

that gives itself in outpouring

joy of rapturous overflowing...

When a creature encounters this Source,

it strengthens

equips them to "complete the story of the world" according to
their role...

Tom is at once Father-less (such is the Father!) ...Logos...

There then is a divinised and transfigured Incarnation – he can
put ON the ring

(as contemplator within exitus and reditus

and Goldberry as the ("post-modern") constant interplay of
wonder and interpretation (Water-Spirit // Ruah over chaos)

Divine Dance/Wisdom/Unceasing

Mystery of Fecund Contemplation

... that which will be in the Beatific Vision (Rublev Icon)...

we through the hobbits are brought into Tom and Goldberry as
Real Presence and Communion,

that which we are drawn into...

links to Tolkien's Eucharistic vision of the mote ... it parallels to
St Julian of Norwich

and the acorn holding totality

Cosmic in the simple;

Hildegard – illumination and life-giving Viriditas… Tom talking
to the "Tree of life"//

a-temporally but incarnate through the song

The broken tree listens still!

… beyond the Fall

(pre-lapsarian innocence

now subsumed in transfiguration beyond poison and glorified!)

Hey! Come merry dol! derry dol! and merry-o!

Goldberry, Goldberry, merry yellow berry-o!

("All shall be well, and all shall be well

and all manner of thing shall be well.")

- Julian of Norwich

It is hoped readers of the poem will respond with their hearts,
minds (psyche) and souls, in accordance with the Truth as they see
it in the depths of their self-awareness, for in purifying our whole
being, we can draw close to the Person and Being of the Spirit of
Tom Bombadil and Goldberry. This process heals us and divinises
us and draws us into the work of the Great Exorcism of the cosmos,
for in healing ourselves we heal the whole human family. In the
movement of the poem we sense that God draws near to those who

listen at the depths of their being, to the new Communion brought about for all who respond generously to Grace. The poem documents this transition from brokenness to Grace as the female protagonist is drawn into the Spirit of Goldberry and in turn the male protagonist is drawn into the Spirit of Tom Bombadil. Their psyches are illuminated and their souls drawn by the Spirit into an innocent and life-giving embrace of listening, openness and generosity which is fruitful.

Goldberry and the healing of heart, mind and spirit

I am a very, very beautiful and powerful woman in a way that I don't understand myself or what to do.

I am untrained in my own self-knowledge, so men drown in me at the bottom of the sea, and I find myself alone.

They drown themselves in me by trying to impress me with themselves.

But they do not see me.

The Real me.

The Me that wants to be known, seen and loved right Now.

Being alone, I am sad at the bottom of the river.

Behold!

On the distance comes a man who has gained the self-knowledge that comes from the Logos.

So, I go to him and my first attempts are to drown him.

He tries to sing to me, but taken unawares he falls to the bottom of the water with me.

And we are drowning, and it feels like agonising death and crushing under crashing, crashing and crashing waves…

Now he does something new;

He takes me home, as he has a home, and listens to me.

After listening to me,

He goes walking out in the world every day and collects me flowers.

The flowers represent his patient contemplation of my fertility.

His trust is as old as time itself.

He sings because he is free.

When I marry him, he rejoices,

And holds my slender middle.

But it plays like a fiddle,

Because the cost of that holding

Is precise as the most precise art of fiddle-playing.

Our Combined Art is innocence;

And it's an innocence as old as time.

And in that innocence The Ring is a mere "trifle."

I am no longer at the bottom of the sea and neither is he,

In our encounter with each other.

In all this, I will only tell you My tale,

If you LISTEN TO ME.

In Tolkien's legendarium, the Ring of Power is a symbol of the evil of having power over another. Mercy, however, is a pathway back to original innocence, and is a truth that Tolkien exposes in his works, which is key to my own advocacy of this story as having psychological significance for the healing of a patient's mind. This story came to me from everything that I have ever learned. It can be read on a spiritual level, or even on a literal level. It is very simple at heart, but I believe it has a power that speaks as loud as the human heart.

CHAPTER 11:

The "Wyrd Wonder" of Tom and Goldberry

Mystical Integration of the Great Story in Tolkien's Play

Cynicism, mercilessness, despair, apathy and parody, these are not the way of the Holy Spirit. In Tolkien's legendarium evil often takes the path down this route and Tolkien's heroes struggle relentlessly in the fray of a "sacral play," so as to overcome these life-sapping abysses. Subsequently hobbits are taken into the tale of such combat against evil, and it is precisely their often-virtuous resilience against all odds that sees them resist and overcome the trappings of the enemy. But why are hobbits from a seemingly quasi-modern age thrown into a smorgasbord of disconnected past ages with all the perhaps whimsical dissonance to achieve this end? This is a question that was levelled at me, quite fairly I think, by Avellina Ballestri, chief editor of *Fellowship and Fairydust*. She worded her contention as follows:

I think I figured out what I don't like more specifically about the LotR world. If it was about a young farm boy from a Dark Ages village in Rohan whose simple life is overthrown by orc attacks, and he goes on to become a great warrior hero to save his loved ones and small village, and ultimately even the world, that would work for me. Same universe. Same consistency. And the flavor of original Anglo-Saxon lore remains steady across the board. Same concept of the meek inheriting the earth. But the hobbit world is from a totally different era, a totally different compartment of English literature and historical reference, so it just feels jolting.

My response to Avellina is rooted in my understanding of what I call "Wyrd wonder," a jolting necessity needed for the artist to breathe life within a living tradition; that allows them to build a future imagined through the wisdom of the past. Wyrd Wonder captivated Shakespeare and also Blake and it was certainly in the heart and mind of the Beowulf poet, who I will use as my example.

Old English *wyrd* is a verbal noun formed from the verb *weorþan*, meaning "to come to pass, to become". The term developed into the modern English adjective *weird*. From the 14th century *to weird* was also used as a verb in Scots, in the sense of *to preordain by decree of fate*. Wyrd is the notion of a transcendent narrative that shaped the unfurling of the world, that was grasped by the pre-Christian mind of the Beowulf poet's oral tradition source as "Fate" rather than the later "Providence of the Creator." Wyrd caused the human mind to wonder at the recurring themes of human nature, allowing an artistic action to embrace a range of historical periods and hold them in unity without dissonance. The Beowulf poet does just this when he mediates his oral traditions; he is bridging the gap between the intangible past of an unrecorded oral tradition and the changing world of a new Christian illumination, written on vellum!

In the Light of a Logos – i.e., the Word of God, or principle of divine reason and creative order, identified in the Gospel of John with the second person of the Trinity incarnate in Jesus Christ - and its revelation for this monk and his scribes, human language takes a transcendence borne from the notion of a Divine revelation, allowing human words to hold eternal meaning. These eternal notions can now dance between the alterity of the past and the new world that is forming, without any artistic conflict. Consider Grendel's descent from Cain and the Scop's (Bard's) singing regarding the Shaper of the cosmos. Here you have the smorgasbord brought together in artistic unity by the skill of the story-teller. Cain is known by omniscient narrator and so we are told of Grendel's origins, but then more than this jolt, even the bard at Heorot knows of the Creator and his shaping. It is possible to overcome the conflagration of time periods, jumping from

Finnsburg fragments to Scyld Scyfing's arrival, because of the lens of the monastic author's understanding of "wyrd wonder" (from Middle English wonder, wunder, from Old English wundor ("wonder, miracle, marvel"), from Proto-Germanic *wundrą); of a fated story where unity is borne from an underlying wondrous principle of the Logos' shaping (Poetry Foundation 2022). In the light of "Wyrd" become "Logos' Providence" it is possible to dance and play between intangible alterity, the becoming of the present, and the imagined destiny or telos of the world in the artist's hope.

The miracle of storytelling is the drawing from the intangible past and bridging the gap with its alterity through the mediatorship of the artist who is caught up or infused with the illumination of "wyrd wonder," and the slowly shaping story of the rolling of time itself into eternity. There is an urgency then to speak at this point in time and to continue the story for those who will listen. In this notion of "wyrd wonder" Tolkien's smorgasbord of time periods can be argued to be a morally necessary unity of art. In such a mystical reading, consider then his existential locus. War, the ravaging of the countryside, the loss of the elves at the turning tide of modernity was then even more jarring than for Richard Corbet almost 400 years earlier. In 1591, the English bishop Richard Corbet had penned a poetic farewell to the elves, which included the lines:

By which we note the fairies

Were of the old Profession.

Their songs were 'Ave Mary's',

Their dances were Procession.

But now, alas, they all are dead;

Or gone beyond the seas; (Bradford 1973)

In the light of the Logos which Tolkien loved, there was a moral duty to bring back the elves so that our future may be grafted to their light. This was not a wild escapist fantasy; this was a moral duty of the artist to connect us to our past so that we might become hobbits in our destiny, incarnating their resilient gentleness, as balrogs and orc-foe and wraiths assail all that we would hold dear, within the continually unfurling play of "Middangeard" (Middle-earth). As one commentator has noted:

Tolkien's is an exquisitely proleptic art that takes a pagan, pre-Christian universe and suffuses it discreetly with a sacramental holiness stemming implicitly from what Balthasar makes bold to call a Christ form. (Sebanc 1993)

Prolepsis is the assigning of a person, event, or thing to a period earlier than the actual one. Both Tolkien and the Beowulf are examples of artists in worlds teetering on the edge of cataclysmic paradigm and cosmological shift; for the Beowulf poet it is Pagan-Christian, for Tolkien it is the emergence into the mundane modernity of nihilism where elves are no longer a serious business and hobbits have nothing meaningful to fulfil. Tolkien takes the creative attack and sends such thinkers an ancient Balrog to viscerally engage (it is already on the bridge!), as the Beowulf poet does with his Grendel. Vehemently through an intentional artistry, he typifies and becomes an apotheosis case of the work of a Bard; in his dance between the liminal realm of the past's alterity and the present. Why? So that the future can belong to the hobbits who can continue a unity with what has come before, a journey and quest which is resilient to its last breath in the Long Defeat, but miraculously suffused by a light that overcomes all evil throws at them. But from where does the light come?

The answer is revealed through the distinct importance of the kneeling to the hobbits in *The Return of the King*. They are the questers for the light old as dawn. They have become suffused by it. "Wyrd Wonder" was always sensed, and it led the hobbits down ancient pasts into a new and glorious vision of the future, as the eagles arrived true to the seeming "luck" of the Logos' interplay in Arda. As Finrod noted in his conversation with Andreth:

For that Arda Healed shall not be Arda Unmarred, but a third thing, and greater and yet the same… To speak according to Time in which they have their being, the Arda Healed, which shall be greater and more fair than the first, because of the Marring: this is the Hope that sustaineth. It cometh not only from the yearning of the Will of Ilúvatar the Begetter (which by itself may lead those within Time to more than regret) but also from trust in Eru the

Lord Everlasting, that he is good and his works shall all end in good. (HME Morgoth's Ring)

As Huizinga states:

What this means is that Tolkien's enchanted world of faerie is best and most fruitfully considered as an ordered, thaumaturgic field of play, set up in a sacral mode, we might almost say, to yield the impression of "distance and a great abyss of time... In the form and function of play, itself an independent entity which is senseless and irrational, man's consciousness that he is embedded in a sacred order of things finds its first, highest, and holiest expression. Gradually the significance of a sacred act permeates the playing. Ritual grafts itself upon it; but the primary thing is and remains play. (Huizinga 2016)

Sacramental vision through mythopoesis is the final synthesis of all the yearning of mythos for Absolute truth, with the emergence of the miracle of the Revelation of Christ as the form of "myth become fact" (Tolkien 2008). In the light of Christian illumination, a duty of continuity now exists between the past elves and the restoration of the elves in the future; one that is so deeply important, that art is not sacrificed by bridging the gap, but rather is saved through the journey to alterity of the past, so that the future can be redeemed through that same wild romance that has brought us to our current and present struggle against timeless evil.

Peter Jackson did not include the Scouring of the Shire or Tom Bombadil in his film trilogy, and if I met him, I would say to him that his trilogy was inspired, but in the *future* let us make a small inclusion in the films of the Scouring of the Shire and the "Wyrd Wonder" of Tom Bombadil, so that it can indeed be scoured true, *for where did Bill the pony run to when all was said and done?* The scouring of the Shire is the thaumaturgic field of play for Western culture down to the detail of Bill being taken in by Tom Bombadil through his memory of gentle times. Let us look then through the alterity of the past and the light of this emerging radiance, at our present and becoming, infused by a mystical knowledge that Tolkien's art sends forth through His understanding that the Logos shines in the darkness, and the darkness has not overcome it (John 1:5).

Hobbits are not a jolting smorgasbord mistake; they are an artistic necessity, that we might learn how to be wise in this very precise moment of our lives, and the future generations of the next ones, and the next ones and the next ones as the "Road goes ever on." In all this, the thaumaturgic Spirit remains most potently, yet gently, in the vitality of Tom Bombadil and Goldberry, perhaps the very source of "wyrd wonder" itself, that new symphony as a mode of being which is the perennial link between every venturer of Middle-earth. In Tom and Goldberry "wyrd wonder" is personified in its apex case. Their Spirit and their Love is a refreshing song, a beauty more ancient than time, yet newer than hatred; in an innocence beyond the hell of evil, though which is peaceful, subtle and a presence of hope; one that awakens the mystical intuition towards the vanquishing of all that stands in the way of the good, the beautiful and the true in every generation.

CHAPTER 12:

"I Will Make All Things New"

The Interior Springtime of Tom and Goldberry as the Basis of the Renewal of Culture

Through myth, through poetry, Tolkien has evoked a feeling beyond words that comes from the deepest levels of our nature, a yearning that God has implanted in us. That feeling is a sign that we are called back to the light. (Caldecott 2012)

When springtime comes, we are filled with joy; it is finally here! Indeed, Blessed John Henry Newman referred to the return of the Catholic Hierarchy to England in the 19th century as a "Second Spring"; the first being the arrival of the Faith through the Augustinian mission in the 6th Century:

The world grows old, but the Church is ever young. She can, in any time, at her Lord's will, "inherit the Gentiles, and inhabit the desolate cities"... "Arise, make haste, my love, my dove, my beautiful one, and come. For the winter is now past, and the rain is over and gone. The flowers have appeared in our land ... the fig-tree hath put forth her green figs; the vines in flower yield their sweet smell. Arise, my love, my beautiful one, and come."... But still could we be surprised, my Fathers and my Brothers, if the winter even now should not yet be quite over? Have we any right to take it strange, if, in this English land, the spring-time of the Church should turn out to be an English spring, an uncertain, anxious time of hope and fear, of joy and suffering, — of bright promise and budding hopes, yet withal, of keen blasts, and cold showers, and sudden storms? (Newman 1852)

The Holy Spirit is renewing the face of the earth. With the arrival of springtime, so too come the gentle splendour of apple blossoms, the magnificence of creamy magnolia and the simple patchwork of a daisy-covered lawn. You may be startled in this month by a blue sky, or caught in silent thought at the playfulness of a morning breeze amongst idle trees. In all this can you not sense the wondrous ecstasy of Tom Bombadil and Goldberry?

With all this surrounding beauty our hearts can be drawn to contemplate the wonder of God's loving care and be refreshed. In the joy of the simple harmony of beautiful sights, we can find both delight and mystery that awakens the best parts of our nature.

In reading Stratford Caldecott's spiritual vision of Tolkien, he, like Tolkien, is a Catholic writer exploring the relationship between truth and beauty. His reflection is about Tolkien's spiritual vision. In it he looks at Tolkien's faith and his writing in the pursuit of truth as a healing process, which he thinks can help society and is worthy of a spiritual springtime meditation that can renew our hearts with gratitude for God's goodness as creation unfurls around us. One of the best sentences in the book – quoted at the top of this chapter - comes about halfway through as he tries to grasp the essence of Tolkien's writings. For Caldecott, this journey back to the light is the singing heart of all Tolkien's legendarium, a light that guides towards final reconciliation. And does the light not find its most powerful expression in the home of Goldberry where she "shuts out the night," and in Tom who in taking the ring, hands it back after laughing and winking? Interestingly, Caldecott makes a link with Tolkien's devotion to the Virgin Mary. He quotes from Tolkien's letters:

I attribute whatever there is of beauty and goodness in my work to the influence of the Holy Mother of God. (Pearce 2022)

Tolkien saw natural things overflowing with a depth of meaning, sourced in the mind of God, and in his view the Virgin was the most perfect of God's creatures. She was the heart of Tolkien's spiritual life, the model for showing us how to be receptive to the light of God's will and his infusing Spirit that gives life to all the cosmos. As Caldecott explains:

But at the feet of Mary the ground is green with grass and bright with flowers ... This is the Mary who is ever-present to Tolkien, at the centre of his imagination, mantled by all-natural beauty. (Caldecott 2012).

Mary is the magnet of the Holy Spirit. Where Mary is, the Holy Spirit is drawn in its fullness to bring forth the Incarnation of *another* Christ in all believers who turn to her assistance. Mary can give a new springtime to our hearts, and she does this in the Spirit of Tom Bombadil and Goldberry. She does this by leading us to the beauty, peace, power and simplicity of her Son, who is the cause and catalyst, by His glorious Death and Resurrection, of the ability to "shut out the night" definitively in this cosmos. The Son who is the "Light of the world" (John 8:12) for whom the whole of creation is made for, and finds its completion in. We can meet her in the rosary and ask her to pray for us with simple faith and trust.

Let us remember her in this springtime of our hearts, in the peaceful sunshine and new choruses of birdsong. Let us remember she who is the way the cosmos is joined to God, and let us, in the Spirit of Tolkien, *"Praise the Lord with all mountains and hills, all orchards and forests, all things that creep and birds on the wing"* (Letter 310).

The desire to renew the liberal arts in this Spirit, can find a spirit of freshness and wild power in the enthusiasm of Pope John Paul

II in his *Letter to Artists* (John Paul II 1999). Western civilisation is grounded in a Trinitarian vision of the human person. In this vision there is an eternal "exitus" (outpouring) and "reditus" (return) from the transcendent Divine Godhead to the human person, grounded in the Logos, aka the Divine Word. The Divine Word is the basis of Western civilisation and its defence of individual human dignity and freedom. It is upon the Logos that Western civilisation has fought the long battle to erect an authentic civilisation of truth and love. Cultivating this model of society has been an authentic Catholic liberal arts movement that has at once been grounded in the philosophical impulses of classical thought, as well as bringing forth new fusions and synthesis with the contemporary philosophies – always in constructive dialogue subordinate to "love" as the final goal. The Catholic vision of the human person grounded in the Blessed Trinity is ultimately inexorable with the flourishing of truth in love of each individual in their unique alterity, which promotes unadulterated freedom and delight, with the Spirit of Tom Bombadil and Goldberry, in beauty as the pinnacle of human culture. St. John Paul II gave us the keys to this vision of a renewed culture when he said that bringing a culture to Christ does not destroy that culture, but rather, beautifies its latent goodness from within (John Paul II 1998).

Drawing from the tradition of John Henry Newman and G.K. Chesterton, who have both contributed to the idea of a Western Roman Catholic liberal arts university formation, the true "amateur" and author Stratford Caldecott has provided both a lens and horizon for understanding the future of Roman Catholic thought beyond the "dead-marshes" of post-modern degeneration and degradation. In his analysis of Tolkien's spiritual vision, routed in the Secret Fire and Flame Imperishable and his thesis on liberal arts formation *Beauty for Truth's Sake*, "Strat" has showed us just how romantic the "new orthodoxy" is and how appealing it would be to a society tired of irrational and soulless discourse (Caldecott 2012, 2017). Stratford's vision, wholly grounded in Tolkien, sees philology and the arts as the touchstone for redeeming the West. It will be through the words of our children and the archetypes and narratives that form their burgeoning consciousness that the soul of Western civilisation will either perish or bud; any budding will be rooted in that vernal mysticism that is so evident in Tom Bombadil and Goldberry's dynamic interplay and rapturous joy; in the prophetic words of Aragorn at the hellish Black Gate:

... but it is not this day. This day we fight! By all that you hold dear on this good Earth, I bid you stand. (LOTR)

And we stand for what other than the joy of freedom at the service of the good, the true and beautiful which Tom and Goldberry so much inspire and rub off upon all who encounter them. Drawing from the romantic and holistic tradition of Newman, Chesterton, Tolkien, and Caldecott, the desire to renew the liberal arts can find a Spirit of freshness and wild power (i.e., the infusing Grace of

226

Tom Bombadil and Goldberry) in the enthusiasm of St. John Paul II in the *Letter to Artists*. To further promote this vision of the rebellion of beauty, truth and goodness perceived in logos and mythos against degeneration, moral apathy and evil, a new model of university must emerge in the West. However, this model must note the "eternal revolution" of Chesterton (Orthodoxy 1908). Such a rebellion against tyranny will be so new it is the oldest – "as the Father is younger than we," for Tom Bombadil is Master and his beloved Goldberry is radiant like distilled light.

To rebel against tyranny, radical individual human flourishing and conquest for truth must be promoted. A J. R. R. Tolkien liberal arts university would be a place of encounter with the wisdom of the ancestors, the elves, dwarves and hobbits, from the very "soup" that was boiled for generations on the stoves of our cultural "home." It is from this daily wisdom, as in the Divine Wisdom that dances in the presence of the Master at the dawn of the cosmos, that the juncture is found for building a holistic vision for the future. In this new emerging West, post-modernity will encounter the reality of the Balrog, and rather than shirk from the tyranny of scepticism at the existence of his fiery demonic whip of slavery, will declare with a voice of eternal youth, "I am a servant of the Secret Fire; you shall not pass!" (LOTR). This wizard's voice in good time will return to the Master of the Secret Fire to speak with His Voice, and at the gentle tidings of Goldberry they will definitively shut out the night. Sufficiently kindled by these sentiments, universities in such a Spirit would be a constant source of renewal and life for the whole human family, and provide the crucial bastion against the raging darkness, where the darkness has not overcome the Light (John 1:5).

References

Academy of the Immaculate, cited in Jonathan Fleischman, Who are you O Immaculate Conception [Blog], 2004. Available URL: https://saintmaximiliankolbe.com/who-are-you-o-immaculate-conception/.

Arcade Fire, *My Body is Cage*, 2007. Available URL: https://genius.com/Arcade-fire-my-body-is-a-cage-lyrics.

Barlow, Hannah, *In the Forest of Tom Bombadil* [video], YouTube, 2016, duration: 12 min 18 sec. Available URL: https://youtu.be/i95mdzDuTvc.

Basso, Ann McCauley, Fair Lady Goldberry, Daughter of the River, *Mythlore*, 27(1), 2008, 139-46.

Beal, Jane, Who is Tom Bombadil? Interpreting the light in Frodo Baggins and the role of Tom Bombadil in the healing of traumatic memory in J.R.R. Tolkien's Lord of the Rings, *Journal of Tolkien Research*, 6(1), 2018. Available URL: https://scholar.valpo.edu/journaloftolkienresearch/vol6/iss1/1/

Bebb, Angela, Pity, Mercy and Empathy: Emotional Weapons for Internal Battles in The Lord of the Rings [Essay], Oklahoma Christian University, 2008.

Beowulf, Poetry Foundation, 2022. Available URL: https://www.poetryfoundation.org/poems/50114/beowulf-modern-english-translation.

Bergoglio, Cardinal Jorge, *Archbishop of Buenos Aires to the education community* [Spanish], 2008.
see also under Pope Francis.

Best, Brandon, Tom Bombadil and Goldberry: Romantic Theology as Revelation in Tolkien's The Lord of the Rings [Abstract], Research Symposium, Cedarville University, 2016. Available URL: https://digitalcommons.cedarville.edu/research_scholarship_symposium/2016/podium_presentations/2/.

Bogstad, Janice M. and Kaveny, Philip E. (eds.), *Picturing Tolkien: Essays on Peter Jackson's Lord of the Rings Trilogy*, McFarland & Co., Jefferson, 2011, 309p.

Bradford, Lee Eden, *The Prescience of Richard Corbett: Observations on "The Fairies' Farewell*," Johns Hopkins University Press, 1973.

Brawley, C., The Fading of the World: Tolkien's Ecology and Loss in The Lord of the Rings, *Journal of the Fantastic in the Arts*, 18(3), 2007, 292-307, 435.

Britt, Robert Roy, First sound waves left imprint on the universe, *Space.com* [website], 12 January 2005. Available URL: https://www.space.com/661-sound-waves-left-imprint-universe.html.

Caldecott, Stratford, *The Power of the Ring: The Spiritual Vision behind the Lord of the Rings*, Independent Publishers Group, 2012.

-----, *Beauty for Truth's Sake: On the Re-enchantment of Education,* Brazos Press 2017.

Callahan, P.J., Tolkien, Beowulf and the Barrow-wights, *Notre Dame English Journal*, 1972.

Campbell, Liam, "The Enigmatic Mr. Bombadil: Tom Bombadil's Role as a Representation of Nature in *The Lord of the Rings*," in *Middle-earth and Beyond: Essays on the World of J.R.R. Tolkien*, ed. Kathleen Dubs and Janka Kascakova (Newcastle: Cambridge Scholars, 2010), 41-65.

-----, *The Ecological Augury in the Works of J.R.R. Tolkien*, Walking Tree, 2011.

Carpenter, Humphrey, *J.R.R. Tolkien – A Biography*, Allen & Unwin, London, 1977.

Carrol, Lewis, *Alice in Wonderland*, Macmillan, London, 1865.

Carswell, John, Why Catholics should embrace Tolkien's Beren and Luthien, *Catholic Exchange* [Blog], 14 June 2017. Available URL: https://catholicexchange.com/joy-beyond-walls-world-catholics-embrace-tolkiens-beren-luthien.

Carter, Charles William., *The Person and Ministry of the Holy Spirit*, Michigan: Baker Book House, 1974.

Carter, Humphrey and Tolkien, Christopher, *The Letters of J.R.R. Tolkien*, Allen & Unwin, 1981.

Catholic Online, Nicene Creed, *Catholic Online* [Website], 2017. Available URL: http://www.catholic.org.

Chesterton, G.K., *Orthodoxy*, 1908. Available URL: https://www.pagebypagebooks.com/Gilbert_K_Chesterton/Orthodoxy/The_Ethics_of_Elfland_p10.html.

-----, *Manalive*, John Lane, London, 1912.

Coffey, David, The whole Rahner on the Supernatural Existential, *Theological Studies*, 65, 2004.

Coldplay, *The Scientist*, 2002. Available URL: https://genius.com/Coldplay-the-scientist-lyrics.

Cook, Jared (a), Enoch and the Silmarillion Part 1: Context and structure of the Tale of Enoch, *By Common Consent* [blog], 24 February 2017. Available URL: https://bycommonconsent.com/2017/02/24/enoch-and-the-silmarillion-part-1-context-and-structure-of-the-tale-of-enoch/.

----- (b), Enoch and the Silmarillion Part IV: The Elves' Weeping Goddess [Nienna], *ibid.*, 8 March 2017. Available URL: https://bycommonconsent.com/2017/03/08/enoch-and-the-silmarillion-part-iv-the-elves-weeping-goddess/.

Craig, W, Reasonable Faith, 2022; Available URL: https://www.reasonablefaith.org/writings/question-answer/necessary-existence-and-the-ontological-argument.

Chrétien, Jean-Louis, *The Call and the Response*, Fordham University Press, 2004.

Davis, Daniel Côté, *Why Some Catholics Think J.R.R. Tolkien Could Be a Saint*, The European Conservative [Blog], 12 March 2022. Available URL: https://europeanconservative.com/articles/essay/why-some-catholics-think-j-r-r-tolkien-could-be-a-saint/#:~:text=Throughout%20his%20life%2C%20Tolkien%20fostered,and%20Divinity%20of%20Jesus%20Christ.

see also under Rutillio, Danny Oscar.

Day, David, *A-Z of Tolkien*, Chancellor Press, London, 1993.

Denney, Jim, The enigma of Tom Bombadil in The Lord of the Rings (parts 1 & 2), *Timebenders* [Blog], 6 July 2012. Available URL: https://jimdenney.wordpress.com/2012/07/05/the-enigma-of-tom-bombadil-in-the-lord-of-the-rings-part-1/.

Dickerson, Mathew, and Evans, Jonathan, *Ents, Elves and Eriador: The Environmental Vision of J.R.R. Tolkien*, University Press of Kentucky, 2006.

Donaghy, Bill, In the House of Tom Bombadil [Blog], Catholic Exchange, 20 October 2006. Available URL: http://catholicexchange.com/in-the-house-of-tom-bombadil.

Duchamp, Marcel, A GUEST + A HOST = A GHOST, Crumpled candy wrapper with black ink on green foil [artwork], William Copley Exhibition, Galerie Nina Dausset, Paris, 1953, Available URL: http://archives.carre.pagesperso-orange.fr/Duchamp%20Marcel.html

Duriez, Colin, *The J.R.R. Tolkien Handbook*, Baker, Grand Rapids, 1992.

Elkington, David, *The Ancient Language of Sacred Sound: The Acoustic Science of the Divine*, Inner Traditions International, 2nd edition, 2021, 432p.

-----, The Ancient Language of Sacred Sound [video], *YouTube*, 8 May 2021, duration: 1.42.40. Available URL: https://youtu.be/pGXsWLRSgxE. Interview with the Cuyamungue Institute.

Encyclopedia of Arda, Tom Bombadil, *Encyclopaedia of Arda* [Website], 14 June 2003. Available URL: http://www.glyphweb.com/arda/t/tombombadil.php.

Enright, Nancy, Tolkien's females and the defining of power, *Renascence*, 59(2), Winter 2007, 93-133.

EWTN, *Discovering Tolkien* [video], Eternal World Television Network, 2018, duration: 60 minutes. Available URL: https://www.ewtnreligiouscatalogue.com/discovering-tolkien-the-lord-of-the-rings-dvd/p/HV000DTD.

Fuller, Edmund, Lord of the Hobbit, in Isaacs and Zimbardo (eds.), *Tolkien and the Critics* ... (1968).

Fanatics Plaza, Tom and the Flame Imperishable, *Fanatics Plaza forum* [Website], 10 June 2004. Available URL: http://www.lotrplaza.com/archives/.

-----, Tom Bombadil = the Flame Imperishable, *Fanatics Plaza forum* [Website], 2005. Available URL: http://www.lotrplaza.com/archives/.

-----, Tom Bombadil's Identity, *Fanatics Plaza forum* [Website], 2012. Available URL: http://www.lotrplaza.com/archives/.

Forget, J., Holy Ghost, *The Catholic Encyclopedia*, 1911. Available URL: http://www.newadvent.org/cathen/07409a.htm.

Forest-Hill, Lynn, "Hey dol, merry dol": Tom Bombadil's Nonsense, or Tolkien's Creative Uncertainty? A Response to Thomas Kullmann, *Connotations: a journal of Critical Debate*, 25(1), 2015/2016, 91-107.

Foster, Robert, *The Complete Guide to Middle-earth*, Ballantine Books, New York, 1978.

Frances, Christy Di, The Central Role of Nature in Tolkien's Christian Myth, *Third Annual Undergraduate Research Symposium*, Charis – The Institute of Wisconsin Lutheran College, 4 May 2003.

Fuller, Molly Brown, The Uncanny and the Postcolonial in J.R.R. Tolkien's Middle-earth, Honors Thesis, University of Central Florida, 2013. Available URL: http://stars.library.ucf.edu/honorstheses1990-2015/1809/.

Gaitley, M., *The One Thing Is Three: How the Most Holy Trinity Explains Everything*, Marian Press, 2012.

Gandalf and Bombadil, *The Tolkien Forum*, 2002-2015. Available URL: https://www.thetolkienforum.com/threads/gandalf-and-bombadil.7100/.

Gandalf on Tom Bombadill, *The Barrow-Downs Discussion Forum*, 2012. Available URL: http://forum.barrowdowns.com/showthread.php?t=18032.

Gay, David Elton, J.R.R. Tolkien and the Kalevala: Thoughts on the Finnish origins of Tom Bombadil and Treebeard, in Jane Chance (ed.), *Tolkien and the Invention of Myth: A Reader*, University Press of Kentucky, 2004, 295-304.

Geekzone, Who and What was Tom Bombadil? [video], *YouTube*, 14 November 2017. Available URL: https://youtu.be/sQgTv5z5O0Q.

Gettier, Edmund, Is Justified True Belief Knowledge?, Analysis, 23, 1963, 966, Available URL: http://fitelson.org/proseminar/gettier.pdf

Gueroult, Denys and Tolkien, J.R.R., Interview [audio], *Reluctant Olympians*, BBC Radio, London, 26 November 1964. Duration: 39.39 minutes. Available URL: https://youtu.be/bzDtmMXJ1B4.

-----, Interview [audio], Recorded Programme Permanent Library, BBC Radio, London, 20 January 1965. Duration [extract]: 11.41 minutes. Available URL: https://youtu.be/yFexwNCYenI.

Greene, Deidre, High argument: Tolkien and the tradition of vision, epic and prophecy, in Patricia Reynolds and Glen H. Goodknight (eds.), *The J.R.R. Tolkien Centenary Conference*, Tolkien Society and Mythopoeic Press, 2003, 45-52.

Hammond, Wayne G. and Scull, Christina, *The Lord of the Rings: A Reader's Companion*, Harper Collins, 2002.

-----, Addenda and Corrigenda to The Adventures of Tom Bombadil and Other Verses from the Red Book (2014), *wayne & christina* [Weblog], 11 April 2018. Available URL: http://www.hammondandscull.com/addenda/bombadil.html.

Hardy, Peter, Mystical Marriage & Meanings of the Cross, 2020. Available URL:. https://vibrantbliss.wordpress.com/2020/03/13/mystical-marriage-meanings-of-the-cross/.

Hargrove, Gene, Who is Tom Bombadil?, *Mythlore*, 47, August 1986. Updated online 1996. Available URL: https://www.cas.unt.edu/~hargrove/bombadil.html.

-----, Who is Tom Bombadil? *The Grey Havens* [Blog], 2016. Available URL: http://www.cas.unt.edu/-hargrove/bombadil.html.

Hartley, Gregory, A Wind from the West: The Role of the Holy Spirit in Tolkien's Middle-earth, *Christianity and Literature*, 62(1), Autumn 2012, 95-120.

Head, Hayden, Imitative Desire in Tolkien's Mythology: A Girardian Perspective, *Mythlore*, 26(1), 2007, 137-148.

Helms, Randel, *Myth, Magic and Meaning in Tolkien's World*, Thames & Hudson, 1974.

-----, *Tolkien and the Silmarils*, Houghton Mifflin, Chicago, 1981.

Hensler, Kevin R., God and Ilúvatar: Tolkien's use of Biblical parallels and tropes in his cosmography, *Mythmoot II: Back Again*, Proceedings of the 2nd Mythgard Institute Mythmoot Conference, Maritime Institute, Linthicum, Maryland, 13-15 December 2013.

Herbert, Gary B., Tolkien's Tom Bombadil and the Platonic Ring of Gyges, *Extrapolation*, Kent State University Press, 26(2), 1985, 152-9.

History of the Ages, Who or what was Tom Bombadil?, *History of the Ages* [YouTube channel], 27 October 2018. Duration: 5.19 minutes. Available URL: https://youtu.be/fvDzanz2HhI.

----- (a), Where could Tom Bombadil have come from?, *History of the Ages* [YouTube channel], 6 January 2021. Duration: 9.01 minutes. Available URL: https://youtu.be/McA6N2ycHjs.

----- (b), Why wasn't Sauron invisible when he wore the one ring?, *History of the Ages* [YouTube channel], 4 January 2021. Duration: 6.34 minutes. Available URL: https://youtu.be/LOp1MpaIfzQ.

Hopkins, Gerard Manley, As Kingfishers Catch Fire, *Gerard Manley Hopkins: Poems and Prose,* Penguin Classics, 1985.

Huizinga, J., *Homo Ludens: A Study of the Play-Element in Culture*, Angelico Press, 2016.

In Deep Geek, Who is Tom Bombadil? [video], *In Deep Geek* [YouTube channel], 15 March 2020. Duration: 10.53 minutes. Available URL: https://youtu.be/jDqYInyet3I.

Internet Encyclopedia of Philosophy, Anselm – Ontological Argument, *IEP* [website], 2022. Available URL: https://iep.utm.edu/anselm-ontological-argument/

Isaacs, Neil D. and Zimbardo, Rose A. (eds.), *Tolkien and the Critics: Essays on J.R.R. Tolkien's The Lord of the Rings*, University of Notre Dame Press, 1968, 296p.

Jackson, Peter (director), *The Fellowship of the Ring*, New Line Cinema, 2001.

-----, *The Two Towers*, New Line Cinema, 2002.

-----, *The Return of the King*, New Line Cinema, 2003.

Jeffs, Carol, A Merry Fellow, *Mallorn: The Journal of the Tolkien Society*, 24, September 1987, 25-27.

Jenike, K., Tom Bombadil – Man of Mystery, in Janka Kaščáková (ed.), *Middle-earth and Beyond: Essays on the World of J.R.R. Tolkien*, Cambridge Scholars Publishing, 2010.

Jensen, Steuard, Bombadil as a Nature Spirit [Blog], *Tolkien Meta-FAQ*, 2001. Available URL: http://tolkien.slimy.com/essays/Bombadil4Spirits.html.

John Paul II, *Letter to Young People*, The Vatican, 1985
    Accessible at: https://www.vatican.va/content/john-paul-ii/en/apost_letters/1985/documents/hf_jp-ii_apl_31031985_dilecti-amici.html.

    -----, *Fides et Ratio*, The Vatican, 1998. Available URL: https://www.vatican.va/content/john-paul-ii/en/encyclicals/documents/hf_jp-ii_enc_14091998_fides-et-ratio.html

    -----, *Letter to Artists*, The Vatican, 1999. Available URL: https://www.vatican.va/content/john-paul-ii/en/letters/1999/documents/hf_jp-ii_let_23041999_artists.html.

Johnson, Sean Aram, *Fog on the Barrow Downs: Celtic Roots of Tolkien's Mythology*, BA thesis, Boston College, 2010, 149p.

Joyce, George, The Blessed Trinity, *The Catholic Encyclopedia*, 15, Robert Appleton Company, New York, 1912. Available URL: http://www.newadvent.org/cathen/15047a.htm.

Julian of Norwich, *Revelations of Divine Love*, Penguin, 1998, 240p.

Karukoski, Dome (director), *Tolkien* [movie], Fox Searchlight Pictures, 2019. Duration: 112 minutes.

Katz, Eric, 'The Rings of Tolkien and Plato: Lessons in Power, Choice and Morality, in Gregory Bassham and Eric Bronson (eds.), *The Lord of the Rings and Philosophy*, Open Court, Chicago, 2003, 5-20.

Kemble, John Mitchell, *The Gospel according to Saint Matthew in Anglo-Saxon and Northumbrian versions synoptically arranged, with collations of the best manuscripts*, Cambridge University Press, 1858. Available URL: https://archive.org/stream/gospelaccordingt00kembrich/gospe laccordingt00kembrich_djvu.txt.

Kilby, Clyde S., *Tolkien & the Silmarillion: A Glimpse at the Man and his World of Myth*, Harold Shore, Wheaton, 1976.

Kimel, Aidan, Ainulindalë: The Secret of the Secret Fire, *Eclectic Orthodoxy* [blog], 19 February 2018. Available URL: https://afkimel.wordpress.com/2018/02/19/ainulindale-the-secret-of-the-secret-fire/.

Klamut, Charles, *Absorbed into the Story: Catholic Themes in Tolkien*, n.p., n.d., 74p.

Kocher, Paul, Ilúvatar and the Secret Fire, *Mythlore*, 12(1), 1985, 36-7.

Korkis, Jim, If at first you don't succeed ... call Peter Jackson, *Jim Hill Media* [blog], 24 June 2003. Available URL: http://jimhillmedia.com/alumni1/b/jim_korkis/archive/2003/0 6/25/1087.aspx.

Kreeft, P, *The Philosophy of Tolkien: The Worldview behind The Lord of the Rings, 2005.*

Lauzon, Daniel, The Adventures of Tom Bombadil [comment], *The J.R.R. Tolkien Estate* [Website], 2017. Available URL: http://www.tolkienestate.com/en/writing/other-tales-and-poetry/the-adventures-of-tom-bombadil-and-other-poetry.html.

Lee, Leslie S., "Allows itself to anything:" Poor Tom Familiarizing and Enacting Chaos in King Lear, *Inquiries Journal*, 1(10), 2009.

Lewis, Paul W., Beorn and Tom Bombadil: A Tale of Two Heroes, *Mythlore*, 25(3/4), Spring/Summer 2007, 145-160. Available URL: https://dc.swosu.edu/mythlore/vol25/iss3/13/.

Lim, Jungmyung, Reading J.R.R. Tolkien's Imperialism under Michel Foucault's Eyes, *The Mirae Journal of English Language and Literature,* 21(4), 2016, 51-72.

Lobdell, Jared, *England and Always: Tolkien's World of the Rings*, Eerdmanns, Grand Rapids, 1981.

-----, *The World of the Rings: Language, Religion, and Adventure in Tolkien,* Open Court, Chicago, 2004.

Lockett, Christopher, In Defense of Tom Bombadil, *it's all narrative* [blog], 26 January 2014. Available URL: https://cjlockett.com/2014/01/26/in-defense-of-tom-bombadil/.

Long, Hannah, In Defense of Tom Bombadil, *Longish: Thoughts on television, literature & culture* [blog], 19 July 2012. Available URL: http://longish95.blogspot.com/2012/07/in-defense-of-tom-bombadil.html.

Loos, William D. B., Who or what was Tom Bombadil?, *The Grey Havens* [Website], 2002. Available URL: http://tolkien.cro.net/else/tombom.html.

Lumen Gentium, Vatican Archives, 1964. Available URL: https://www.vatican.va/archive/hist_councils/ii_vatican_coun cil/documents/vat-ii_const_19641121_lumen-gentium_en.html.

Maggie, In Defense of Tom Bombadil, *Thoughts, Words, Deeds, Actions* [blog], 27 November 2011. Available URL: https://maggieflynn49.wordpress.com/2011/11/27/in-defense-of-tom-bombadil/.

Martin, Dawn, Tom Bombadil and Treebeard: the adaptation of Medieval concepts of nature in J.R.R. Tolkien's The Lord of the Rings [Abstract], The C.S. Lewis & Friends Colloquium, Taylor University, 2012. Available URL: https://pillars.taylor.edu/cslfc/2012/program/23/.

Martin, Keith, Oldest and fatherless: the terrible secret of Tom Bombadil, *Loose Connections* [Blog], 20 February 2011. Available URL: http://km-515.livejournal.com/1042.html.

Martin, Thomas L., God and Laughter: Overcoming the Darkness in Modern Fantasy Literature, *North Wind: A Journal of George Macdonald Studies*, 34, 2015. Available URL: https://digitalcommons.snc.edu/northwind/vol34/iss1/1/.

Martinez, Michael, What is Tom Bombadil?, *Middle-earth & J.R.R. Tolkien blog*, 10 November 2011. Available URL: http://middle-earth.xenite.org/what-is-tom-bombadil/.

-----, Why is Tom Bombadil always left out?, *Middle-earth & J.R.R. Tolkien blog*, 10 November 2011. Available URL: http://middle-earth.xenite.org/why-is-tom-bombadil-always-left-out/.

-----, Why did Peter Jackson leave out Tom Bombadil?, *Middle-earth & J.R.R. Tolkien blog*, 10 November 2011. Available URL: http://middle-earth.xenite.org/why-did-peter-jackson-leave-out-tom-bombadil/.

-----, If only I had a Bombadil, *Middle-earth & J.R.R. Tolkien blog*, 4 March 2013. Available URL: http://middle-earth.xenite.org/if-i-only-had-a-bombadil/.

Mathison, Keith, The Bombadil Enigma, *Light in dark places: Reflections on truth, goodness, and beauty* [blog], 16 June 2020. Available URL: https://www.keithmathison.org/post/the-bombadil-enigma.

McIntosh, Jonathan S., Trinity in Middle-earth, parts 1-4, 24 September 2011, *The Flame Imperishable* [Blog]. Available URL: https://jonathansmcintosh.wordpress.com/.

McMurray, Stephen, Enoch's encounters with extraterrestrials, *Nexus: The Alternative News Magazine*, 28(2), February-March 2021, 57-63.

Men of the West, Tom Bombadil – Epic Character History [video], *YouTube*, 23 July 2017. Available URL: https://youtu.be/UrFaRYJ7sSw.

Middle-earth Lore, Why Tom Bombadil and Goldberry aren't in the films, Middle-earth Lore, 12 February 2019. Duration: 3.15 minutes. Available URL: https://youtu.be/AHLnNhHAZ4c.

Minwoo, Yoon, Nature in Tolkien's Literature: The Economy of Slowness, *Medieval and Early Modern English Studies*, 21(1), 2013, 127-157.

Monteiro, F.P., Tom Bombadil, a character out of place: literature as construction of social meanings, *Revista Historia-Debates E Tendencias*, 12(2), 2012, 260-77.

Moxon, David, Fundamentally religious and Catholic, *L'Osservatore Romano*, 31 January 2014. Available URL: http://www.ewtn.com.

Murray, T.A. (ed.), *The Romance and Prophecies of Thomas of Erceldoune*, Early English Text Society, 61, 1875.

Nathan, Ban the Bombadil, *VoVatia* [blog], 3 January 2015. Available URL: https://vovatia.wordpress.com/2015/01/03/ban-the-bombadil/.

Nerd of the Rings, The Complete Travels of Gandalf [video], *Nerd of the Rings*, 25 October 2020. Available URL: https://youtu.be/103qp-p37IE.

-----, Five Great Tom Bombadil Theories [video], *Nerd of the Rings*, 10 January 2021. Duration: 22.20 minutes. Available URL: https://youtu.be/mw9uKzy4GRs.

Newman, Cardinal John Henry, *Sermon 10: The Second Spring*, 1852, Accessible URL: https://www.newmanreader.org/works/occasions/sermon10.html.

Noad, Charles E., The Natures of Tom Bombadil: A Summary, *Tolkien and the Invention of Myth: A Reader*, University Press of Kentucky, 2004, 79-83.

Noetzal, Justin T., Beorn and Bombadil: Mythology, Place and Landscape in Middle-earth, in Lee Eden Bradford (editor), *The Hobbit and Tolkien's Mythology*, McFarland and Co., 2014, 161-80.

Not All Those Who Wander Art Lost, Was Tom Bombadil important to [The Lord of the Rings], *Not All Those Who Wander Art Lost* [Online forum], 16 May 2004. Available URL: http://www.planet-tolkien.com/board/5/2084/0/was-tom-bombadil-important-to-.

O'Neil, Timothy R., *The Individuated Hobbit: Jung, Tolkien and the Archetypes of Middle-earth*, Houghton Mifflin Company, Boston, 1979, 200p.

Ordo Baptismi Parvulorum, 1962, Available URL:
http://www.preces-latinae.org/thesaurus/OBap1962.html.

Organ, Michael, *Tom Bombadil: Tolkien's God on Middle-earth – Deliberate Discordance in The Lord of the Rings*, unpublished manuscript, 2019, 128p.

Panek, Joseph, Tom Bombadil - Nature Spirit (4 parts), *A Seeker's Thoughts* [Blog], 3 April 2011. Available URL: http://www.aseekersthoughts.com.

Parvulesco, Marcel, Things I have learned from Jordan Peterson, Vandal Press [Blog], 26 January 2018. Available URL: https://medium.com/vandal-press/10-things-i-learned-from-jordan-peterson-b54341559fc4.

Pearce, Joseph, Tolkien and Lewis on the Blessed Virgin Mary, *The Imaginative Conservative* [Blog], 8 June 2022. Available URL: https://theimaginativeconservative.org/2022/06/tolkien-lewis-blessed-virgin-mary-joseph-pearce.html.

Penny Catechism, reprint edition, Tan Books, 2009.

Perkins, Agnes and Helen Hill, The Corruption of Power, in Jared Lobdell (ed.), *A Tolkien Compass*, Open Court, La Salle, 1975, 57-68.

Peterson, Jordan, *Biblical Series XI - The Call of Abraham*, 2017, Accessible URL: https://www.youtube.com/watch?v=GmuzUZTJ0GA.

-----, What is logos?, Reddit, 2017. Available URL: https://www.reddit.com/r/JordanPeterson/comments/6cxwh1/what_is_logos_eli5/.

Polanca, R, *Understanding Von Balthasar's Trilogy*, Pontifical University of Chile, 2017.

Pope Francis, *Message of Pope Francis for the 52nd World Day of Prayer for Vocations - Theme: Exodus, a fundamental experience of vocation*, The Vatican, 2015.

-----, *Weaving the World*, Salani Productions, 2022.

see also under Cardinal Jorge Mario Bergoglio.

Pope John Paul II, see under John Paul II.

Popova, Mary, J.R.R. Tolkien reads from The Lord of the Rings [audio file], *Soundcloud*, 2016. Available URL: https://soundcloud.com/brainpicker/jrr-tolkien-reads-from-the-lord-of-the-rings.

Price, Sarah Frances, The Lord of the Sagas: Tolkien's Tom Bombadil and his relation to the Icelandic Saga, Carleton College, 2013.

Prokhorova, Natalia, *The Almost Unpublished Letters of J.R.R. Tolkien*, mss., 2012, 81p.

Quora, Hypothesis: Tom Bombadil is the Dalai Lama of Middle-earth. Discuss, *Quora* [Online forum], October 2015. Available URL: https://www.quora.com/Hypothesis-Tom-Bombadil-is-the-Dalai-Lama-of-Middle-Earth-Discuss.

Ranger from the North, Who is Tom Bombadil - The Case Against: Nature Spirit, *Ranger from the North* [Blog], 9 January 2013. Available URL: http://whoistombombadil.blogspot.com.au/2013/01/the-case-against-nature-spirit.html.

Reilly, Robert J., Tolkien and the Fairy Story., in Neil D. Isaacs and Rose A. Zimbardo (eds.), *Tolkien and The Critics: Essays on J.R.R. Tolkien's The Lord of the Rings*, University of Notre Dame, 1968, 128-50.

Reynolds, Patricia, The Real Tom Bombadil, in *Leaves from the Tree: J.R.R. Tolkien's shorter fiction*, Tolkien Society, London, 1991, 85-8.

RJH, Tolkien: Tom Bombadil as God, *By Common Consent* [blog], 8 May 2013. Available URL: https://bycommonconsent.com/2013/05/08/tolkien-tom-bombadil-as-god/.

robnkarla, The Intoxicating Influence of Tom Bombadil [video], *YouTube*, 24 March 2009. Available URL: https://youtu.be/ZZouiWmzWoY.

Rogers, Greta, Iarwain Ben-adar on the Road to Faerie: Tom Bombadil's Recovery of Premodern Fantasy Values, Master of Arts in English thesis, Liberty University, 2018. Available URL: https://digitalcommons.liberty.edu/masters/489/.

Roman Missal, 2010, Available URL: http://www.liturgies.net/Liturgies/Catholic/roman_missal/eastervigil.htm

Rosebury, B., *Tolkien: A Cultural Phenomenon*, New York: Palgrave Macmillan, 2003.

Rowling, J.K., *Harry Potter and the Deathly Hallows*, Bloomsbury, London, 2007, 607p.

Rublev, Andrei, *Image and explanation of icon of the Trinity*, 2017. Available URL: https://d2y1pz2y630308.cloudfront.net/17509/documents/2017/8/Trinityicon.pdf.

Rutillio, Danny Oscar, "Wyrd Wonder": Mystical Integration of the Great Story in Tolkien's Play, *Fellowship and Fairydust* [Blog], Côté Davis, D, 2021, Available URL: https://fellowshipandfairydust.com/2021/01/26/wyrd-wonder-mystical-integration-of-the-great-story-in-tolkiens-play/.

Saward, John, Morrill, John and Tomko, Michael, *Firmly I Believe and Truly: The Spiritual Tradition of Catholic England*, Oxford University Press, Oxford, 2013, 789p.

Scheps, Walter, The Fairy-tale Morality of The Lord of the Rings, in Jared Lobdell (ed.), *A Tolkien Compass*, Open Court, La Salle, 1975, 43-56.

Science Fiction & Fantasy, Who or what was Tom Bombadil?, *Science Fiction & Fantasy* [blog], 3 February 2011. Available URL: http://scifi.stackexchange.com/.

-----, Who's older: Treebeard or Tom Bombadil, *Science Fiction & Fantasy* [Blog], 14 February 2017. Available URL: https://scifi.stackexchange.com/questions/11019/whos-older-treebeard-or-tom-bombadil.

Scull, Christina, Tom Bombadil and The Lord of the Rings, in *Leaves from the Tree: J.R.R. Tolkien's shorter fiction*, Tolkien Society, London, 1991, 73-7.

----- and Hammond, Wayne, G., *The J.R.R. Tolkien Companion and Guide – 1. Reader's Guide*, Harper Collins, London, 2006.

Sebanc, M., Lover of the Logos, 1993. Available URL: https://www.communio-icr.com/files/sebanc20-1.pdf.

Serebryakova, Natalya (director), *Khraniteli [Keepers of the Ring]*, Leningrad Television, 13 April 1991. Duration: 115 minutes. Available URL: https://youtu.be/NchKygxHw6Q [Part 1]; https://youtu.be/YeAqETtdSeA [Part 2].

Seth, Priya, Tom Bombadil: Cracking the 'Enigma' Code, *Priyasethtolkienfan* [blog], 17 October 2015. Available URL: https://priyasethtolkienfan.wordpress.com/.

-----, Goldberry: The Enigmatic Mrs Bombadil, *Priyasethtolkienfan* [blog], 16 January 2017. Available URL: https://priyasethtolkienfan.wordpress.com/.

Siewers, Alfred K., Tolkien's Cosmic-Christian Ecology: The Medieval Underpinnings, in Jane Chance and Alfred K. Siewers (editors), *Tolkien's Modern Middle Ages*, Palgrave Macmillan, 2008, 139-53.

Shippey, Tom, *J.R.R. Tolkien: Author of the Century*, Houghton Mifflin Co., Boston, 2000.

-----. *The Road to Middle-earth*, Houghton Mifflin Co., Boston, 2003.

Slethaug, G.E., Tolkien, Tom Bombadil and Creative Imagination, *English Studies in Canada*, 4(3), 1978, 341-50.

Snerdley, Thomas, Why do the Black Riders not follow Frodo into the Old Forest? Were they in some way scared of Tom Bombadil?, *Quora*, 20 November 2017. Available URL: https://www.quora.com/Why-do-the-Black-Riders-not-follow-Frodo-into-the-Old-Forest-Were-they-in-some-way-scared-of-Tom-Bombadil.

Specks, Patricia Meyer, Power and Meaning in The Lord of the Rings, in Neil D. Isaacs and Rose A. Zimbardo (eds.), *Tolkien and The Critics: Essays on J.R.R. Tolkien's The Lord of the Rings*, University of Notre Dame, 1968, 81-99.

Stanton, Michael N., *Hobbits, Elves and Wizards: Exploring the wonders and worlds of J.R.R. Tolkien's The Lord of the Rings*, New York: Palgrave Macmillan, 2001.

Stevenson, Jeffrey, T.B. or not T.B.: That is the Question, *Amon Hen*, November 2006.

Swank, Kris, Tom Bombadil's last song: Tolkien's "Once upon a time", *Tolkien Studies*, 10, 2013.

Taylor, Taryne Jade, Investigating the Role and Origin of Goldberry in Tolkien's Mythology, *Mythlore: A Journal of J.R.R. Tolkien, C.S. Lewis, Charles Williams, and Mythopoeic Literature*, 27(1), 2008, 147-156.

The Exploring Series, Exploring Middle-earth: Tom Bombadil [video], *YouTube*, 13 February 2017. Available URL: https://youtu.be/CxyYvHkmyxA.

The One Ring, The Blessed Trinity in Letter 131, *The One Ring* [Online forum], 14 October 2003. Available URL: http://forums.theonering.com/viewtopic.php?f=27&t=72329.

Tolkien, Christopher (editor), *The History of Middle-earth*, Allen & Unwin, London, 1983-96. Comprises: 1. The Book of Lost Tales 1 (1983); 2. The Book of Lost Tales 2 (1984); 3. The Lays of Beleriand (1985); 4. The Shaping of Middle-earth (1986); 5. The Lost Road and Other Writings (1987); 6. The Return of the Shadow (The History of The Lord of the Rings v.1) (1988); 7. The Treason of Isengard (The History of The Lord of the Rings v.2) (1989); 8. The War of the Ring (The History of The Lord of the Rings v.3) (1990); 9. Sauron

Defeated (includes The History of The Lord of the Rings v.4) (1992); 10. Morgoth's Ring (The Later Silmarillion v.1) (1993); 11. The War of the Jewels (The Later Silmarillion v.2) (1994); 12. The Peoples of Middle-earth (1996).

Tolkien, J.R.R., Qenya [Quenya] Lexicon, mss., 1915. Updated edition by Helge K. Fauskanger, 25 December 2008. Available URL: http://folk.uib.no/hnohf/Quettaparma.pdf.

-----, The Adventures of Tom Bombadil, *Oxford Magazine*, 52(13), 15 February 1934, 464-5.

-----, *The Hobbit*, George Allen & Unwin, London, 1937.

-----, Leaf by Niggle, *Dublin Review*, 1945.

-----, *The Lord of the Rings*, George Allen & Unwin, London, 3 volumes, 1954-5. All references are to the single volume edition, Harper Collins, London, 1998.

-----(a), *The Adventures of Tom Bombadil and other verses from The Red Book*, George Allen & Unwin, London, 1962.

-----(b), *Ancrene Wisse: The English Text of the Ancrene Riwle*, Early English Text Society, Original Series No. 249, Oxford University Press, London, 1962. Translation by J.R.R. Tolkien.

-----, Once upon a time [poem], in Caroline Hunter (editor), *Winter's Tales for Children 1*, Macmillan, London, 1965, 44-5.

-----, *The Tolkien Reader*, Ballantine, New York, 1966.

-----, J.R.R. Tolkien discussing the Lord of the Rings (c.1968) [audio file], *YouTube*. Duration: 11.41 minutes. Available URL: https://youtu.be/yFexwNCYenI.

-----, *The Silmarillion*, Allen & Unwin, London, 1977. Edited by Christopher Tolkien.

-----, *Unfinished Tales of Númenor and Middle-earth*, Allen & Unwin, London, 1980.

-----, On Fairy-Stories, *Tolkien on Fairy-Stories*. Ed. Verlyn Flieger and Douglas A. Anderson. London: HarperCollins, 2008.

-----, *The Adventures of Tom Bombadil and other verses from The Red Book*, Allen & Unwin, 2014, 298p. Edited by Christina Scull and Wayne G. Hammond.

Tolkien Enterprise, *The Lord of the Rings – Shadows of Angmar* [Computer game], Tolkien Enterprises, 2007.

Tolkien Fans, Catholic themes in The Lord of the Rings?, *Tolkien Fans* [Online forum], 17 December 2013. Available URL: http://www.reddit.com/r/tolkienfans/.

Tolkien Gateway, Tom Bombadil, *Tolkien Gateway* [Blog], 2012. Available URL: http://tolkiengateway.net/wiki/Tom_Bombadil.

-----, Ilúvatar, *Tolkien Gateway* [Blog], 28 July 2017. Available URL: http://tolkiengateway.net/wiki/Ilúvatar.

Tom Bombadil: Defence of the Old Forest, *Minas Tirith Evening Star*, American Tolkien Society, 9(11), 1980.

Treschow, Michael and Duckworth, Mark, Bombadil's Role in The Lord of the Rings, *Mythlore*, 25(1/2), Winter 2006, 175-196. Available URL: https://dc.swosu.edu/mythlore/vol25/iss1/13/.

Vaccaro, Christopher (editor), *The Body in Tolkien's Legendarium: Essays on Middle-earth Corporeality*, McFarland & Co., Jefferson, 2013, 200p.

van de Loo, Joost (a), *Finding Tom Bombadil* [film], Netherlands, 2019. Duration: 45m 52s. Available URL: https://filmfreeway.com/FindingTomBombadil.

----- (b), Finding Tom Bombadil - Interview with Joost van de Loo | Imagine Film Festival 2019, YouTube, 15 March 2019, duration: 3.59 minutes. Available URL: https://www.youtube.com/watch?v=ShIDXvZTsNc&t=40s.

von Balthasar, Hans Urs, Theo-Drama, volume 3: *Theological Dramatic Theory: The Dramatis Personae: Persons in Christ*, in *Theological Trilogy*, 16 volumes, 1993.

Wainwright, Arthur W., *The Trinity in the New Testament*, London: William Climes & Sons, 1962.

What did Gandalf go to Bombadill to talk about in at the end of the third book?, *Reddit Discussion Forum*, 2016-2021. Available URL: https://www.reddit.com/r/tolkienfans/comments/3b32y8/what _did_gandalf_go_to_bombadill_to_talk_about_in/.

What does Gandalf intend to chat with Tom Bombadil about?, *Science Fiction & Fantasy Forum*, 2015. Available URL: https://scifi.stackexchange.com/questions/103380/what-does-gandalf-intend-to-chat-with-tom-bombadil-about.

Williams, Stan, 20 Ways The Lord of the Rings is both Christian and Catholic, *Catholic Education* [Website], January 2003. Available URL: http://www.catholiceducation.org.

Winter, Stephen C., Ho, Tom Bombadil! The hobbits meet a strange wonder in the Old Forest, *Wisdom from the Lord of the Rings* [blog], 3 July 2020. Available URL: https://stephencwinter.com/2020/07/03/.

Zemmour, Corinne, Tolkien in the Land of Arthur: the Old Forest episode from *The Lord of the Rings*, *Mythlore: A Journal of J.R.R. Tolkien, C.S. Lewis, Charles Williams, and Mythopoeic Literature*: 24(3), 2006, 135-163.

Zuidervaart, Lambert, *Balthasar and The Contemplation of Truth*, in Lambert Zuidervaart (ed.), *Truth Matters,* McGill Queen's University Press, Montreal, 2013.

Printed in Great Britain
by Amazon